Battered Love

OVERTURES TO BIBLICAL THEOLOGY

BATTERED LOVE

*Marriage, Sex, and Violence
in the Hebrew Prophets*

RENITA J. WEEMS

FORTRESS PRESS | MINNEAPOLIS

BATTERED LOVE
Marriage, Sex, and Violence in the Hebrew Prophets

Cover graphic: Mary Reed Daniel, "Nature Study No. 20," acrylic on paper, 1980. By permission of the Evans-Tibbs Collection, Washington, D.C.
Cover design: Patricia M. Boman
Author photo: Billy Kingsley

Library of Congress Cataloging-in-Publication Data

Weems, Renita J., 1954–
    Battered love : marriage, sex, and violence in the Hebrew prophets
/ by Renita J. Weems.
       p.   cm.
    Includes bibliographical references and index.
    ISBN 0-8006-2948-5 (alk. paper)
    1. Bible. O.T. Prophets— Criticism, interpretation, etc.
2. Violence in the Bible.   3. Sex in the Bible.   4. Women in the
Bible.   I. Title.
BS1505.2.W38   1995
224'.066—dc20
                                95-39305
                                    CIP

Manufactured in the U.S.A.   AF 1-2948
                                    6   7   8   9   10

In memory of
my grandmothers,
Mary Brown Weems (1906-1947)
and
Lou Willie Clark Baker (1910-1949)

—headragged generals, they were—

Contents

Editor's Foreword

In one of the early volumes of Overtures to Biblical Theology, and one of its finest and most enduring, Phyllis Trible anticipated much of the subsequent conversation about the Bible and critical feminist thought. In *God and the Rhetoric of Sexuality* she introduced important methodological questions and possibilities while insisting, against much feminism that found the Bible hopelessly patriarchal, that it is the concreteness of the text and its specific rhetoric that must concern us.

It is a long way from Phyllis Trible in 1978 to Renita Weems in 1995. A great deal has happened concerning method in scripture study, and a great deal has happened as well in the development of critical feminism. We now are much more self-conscious about the connections between speech, power, and social reality. It is likely, moreover, that neither Trible nor Weems would like to be held too closely to the work of the other. Nonetheless, for all their differences of perspective and methodology, the two authors share an agenda and much more. I am glad that Overtures has been one arena for the development of this important discussion.

It was Trible who invited serious and sustained reflection on metaphor as a primary mode of biblical articulation. Indeed, Cynthia Ozick in *Memory and Metaphor,* has suggested more recently that metaphor belongs characteristically and definitionally to Jewish modes of discourse. Trible's most influential and perhaps most successful study in her groundbreaking work concerned the "womb-like" compassion (*rḥm*) of Yahweh. For many reasons, critical biblical feminism has turned to the problematic and distinctive elements of Yahweh as voice in metaphor. And so Renita Weems, at a far reach from Trible, has explored the capacity of sexist metaphors and images to authorize and legitimate sexist human power. Weems does not hold so intensely and determinedly to the specificity of the text as does Trible, but she is willing to consider the political spin-offs that such trenchant textual voices produce in public practice.

The other venturesome aspect of Weems's work that moves beyond the text itself is her consideration of the problematic of Israel's God, a problematic evidenced in but not contained by rhetoric. Weems's work both moves from Trible's and ventures well beyond it in seeing that the plurivocity of the text is intrinsic to Israel's God-speech. The core critical finding of feminism makes clear that there is no monodimensional voicing of God in the text of ancient Israel, and so most conventional modes of theological articulation are oddly incommensurate with and inadequate to the textual witness itself. Thus, Weems shows that feminist questions are not simply about the problem of "theological masculinity." More profoundly, they concern the entire prospect of theological reflection in anything like our habitual modes.

Weems is here breaking new ground and advancing the argument in important ways. While daring in some of her insights, Weems is in the mainstream of an irreversible move that lodges interpretation in the midst of power. The irreversible quality of her insights concerns the growing, relentless awareness that we shall never again be "innocent." At the time of the assassination of President John F. Kennedy, Patrick Moynihan, then a member of the administration, commented on the mood of the country in light of that death. Said Moynihan, "We shall laugh again, but we

shall never be young again." The current interpretive develop-
ments, of which Weems is an important part, make clear that we
shall never be young—or innocent—again in our reading. The
trade-off, however, may be that we shall laugh! Perhaps we shall
not only laugh again, but perhaps for the first time laugh the
Easter laugh, a laugh about newness wrought by this strange
God who breaks all our expectations and makes all things new.
This will be a laugh of power recognized, of speech emanci-
pated, and of faith made genuinely unencumbered. That, of
course, is a great deal to expect from "reading." But as Weems
knows, and Trible before her, "reading"—informed, attentive,
sustained, passionate, increasingly "odd"—is the way our
Jewish forebears have come always again to recognition, eman-
cipation, and unencumberment. Weems here does a great deal
to move us past "youngness" and on toward a new laugh that we
have never before dared.

—Walter Brueggemann

Acknowledgments

When I began my curious obsession with the topic of sexual violence as a poetic portrayal of divine retribution, I had frequently to defend my interest in the topic against skeptics who claimed, "It's only a metaphor." Now, ten years later, the climate has changed. Audiences are keen to learn about the influence of sex and violence on the cultural imagination. And even though I suspected then that sexual violence in poetic texts deserved further scrutiny, I cannot say that I had any clue where the topic would ultimately lead. I have grown, as has my understanding of sex and violence. This volume contains a profoundly different understanding from what began ten years ago when in Princeton Theological Seminary's library I fortuitously stumbled upon an article entitled "Of Rape and Judgment," published in a 1985 issue of *Daughters of Sarah*. The article on sexual violence in the scriptures catapulted me on this journey, and I wish to thank the author (whom I have never actually met), Gracia Faye Ellwood, for writing such a fine piece.

Others have contributed greatly to my work over the years on the topic of sex and violence in prophetic discourse, and they deserve to be thanked publicly. My interlocutors at Princeton Theological Seminary stood firmly behind me throughout my study, and I am grateful. Once I left Princeton, however, one person in particular played an important role as a sounding board in my struggles to teach myself newer critical methods (e.g., reading theories, literary criticism, and ideological criticism) and thereby to reinvent myself as an exegete. Mary Ann Tolbert, formerly a colleague here at Vanderbilt University Divinity School, now on the faculty of the Graduate Theological Union, proved to be the sort of senior faculty colleague every junior faculty person needs: she was a good listener to all my troubles with teaching, writing, and trying to be a responsible womanist/feminist. A brilliant theorist and a daily feminist, Mary Ann helped me to think aloud about what I was trying to do. I am grateful for all the time she spent patiently midwifing me into a new way of reading biblical texts. Of course, Mary Ann is not to be blamed for whatever faulty thinking may show up on the pages of this book. That blame can rest squarely on the shoulders of the author.

Other colleagues here at Vanderbilt, especially Sallie McFague and Doug Knight, have been a tremendous source of encouragement when I've felt I was running out of steam. I am also grateful for grants from both the University Research Council of Vanderbilt University and the Association of Theological Schools (Young Scholars Program), which made it possible for me to write, write, and rewrite this book.

Womanist colleagues across the country for the last year have sent me sisterly messages through the internet that history deserves to know about. Historiographers years from now should know that those black women who first pioneered in their theological disciplines during the last decades of the twentieth century supported each other and formed for themselves a not-so-secret underground community. Katie G. Cannon, Cheryl Townsend Gilkes, Emilie M. Townes, Gay Byron, and Kelly Brown Douglas have been friends and colleagues in the best sense of the word.

Sitting here in my study this morning with the pages of this manuscript strewn about my feet, I would have collapsed under the weight of this project had I not had the fine editorial support of Michael West at Fortress Press. I appreciate the care that he and the entire Fortress Press staff have taken to develop this book. I want also to thank Walter Brueggemann, editor of the Overtures to Biblical Theology series, who read this manuscript in an earlier version and, based on that stumbling version of the manuscript, welcomed its inclusion in OBT. One of my students, Alice Hudiburg, pitched in at the last minute to help edit the final manuscript and bring some uniformity to its scattered pieces. I want to thank her for her labors.

Moreover, I want to thank my family for bearing with me through this entire project. I thank my husband, Martin L. Espinosa, for proving to be a highly adaptable man and finding the challenge of living with "one of those writing women" an interesting research project in itself. Savannah, our daughter, patiently shared her mother with the computer in her mother's study; and when she could stand it no longer she promptly plopped her two-year-old bottom in her mother's lap and insisted on finishing my sentences for me on the computer. Thank you, sweetheart, I couldn't have said it better myself.

Finally, I dedicate this volume to the memory of my maternal and paternal grandmothers, Marie Brown Weems and Lou Willie Clark Baker, both of whom died before I was born. It is fitting to dedicate this book about sex and violence in biblical texts to two women whose deaths were the result of the enormous burden they bore as God-fearing African American women living in the South during the first half of the twentieth century. The official cause of death in the case of my paternal grandmother, Marie Brown Weems, was tuberculosis. But she actually died, say my father and others who knew her, from giving birth to lots of babies in substandard living conditions. My mother's mother, Lou Willie Clark Baker, died from a gunshot wound intended for one of her sons. She, like the poeticized wife in the prophets' speeches, was a victim of a battle between men. This book is dedicated to them as a way of letting them know, should they be listening, that their lives and deaths were more than just metaphors in my family history. As unmentionable as may be some of the details of their lives and deaths, nevertheless, Marie Brown Weems and Lou Willie Clark Baker were real women with real dreams. One of their dreams has exceeded their wildest imaginations: they are grandmothers to a woman with a room of her own.

Introduction
A Metaphor's Fatal Attraction

What in the image of a naked, mangled female body grips the religious imagination? What can humiliating women and mutilating their bodies have to do with talk about God's love for a people? Why do demagogues appeal to sexual images to frame what they have to say about political anarchy and religious idolatry? These are just a few of the questions that motivated the present volume. I have for a long time been intrigued by the ways in which human sexuality is imagined in biblical rhetoric. This project originated in what struck me as the puzzling ways in which divine love, compassion, commitment, reconciliation—otherwise irresistibly sentimental themes—became associated with battery, infidelity, and the rape and mutilation of women.

I began my inquiry into biblical representations of female sexuality with prophetic speeches in the Hebrew Bible. Here one finds conscious attempts to draw analogies between Israel's social and political predicament and the fate of promiscuous, headstrong women. While sexual imagery appears in virtually all the prophetic books, three prophets in particular stand out for their ribald descriptions of promiscuous women.[1] Commentators frequently note the ways in which elaborate descriptions of naked, battered women's bodies function in the prophecies of Hosea, Jeremiah, and Ezekiel as a poetic device for discussing divine punishment and social anarchy. Inveighing, as prophets normally did, against the official practices of the religious and political establishments, all three used imagery associated with bodily functions, particularly those related to female sexuality, to denounce public policies they thought profane and perilous. The prophet Hosea cast portions of his eighth-century commentary in the form of a marital feud between a husband and wife, the former hurling accusations and threats against a wife he perceived to be sexually loose and morally intractable. The prophet Jeremiah sprinkled his prophecies with descriptions of a loose, wanton woman who was dressed in apparel befitting only a whore and whose fate was sure to be that of a whore. Ezekiel devoted two full chapters to narrating the sordid demise of a once-beautiful paramour, contrasting her past fame to her present sexual degradation. By portraying women variously as the sexually promiscuous wife, the brazen whore, and the mutilated paramour, the prophets were hoping to arouse in their audiences the kinds of emotions that would help underscore their messages of doom—emotions of disgust, contempt, terror, and shame.

The aim of this project is to examine how popular norms and attitudes about women, their bodies and sexuality, lent themselves to manipulation and exploitation by the prophets as they sought to win their male audience to a certain way of thinking. We want to see how the prophets combined topics of marriage, sex, and violence into a powerful rhetoric of dread and desire. The intention is to consider first how and why violence seems to be an inevitable component in the prophets' representation of women, sex, and marriage.[2] We want, second, to consider how romance and violence are combined in prophetic rhetoric so as to both fascinate and repel audiences.

Violence against women in the Bible is virtually always cast in sexual terms. Women are punished with rape, beatings, exposure of their private parts, and mutilation of their bodies—and often these things take place at hands of men who are related to them (e.g., Jephthah's daughter in Judges 13; the virgin daughter of Gibeah and the Levite's concubine in Judges 19; or Tamar in 2 Samuel 13). The correlation drawn repeatedly in prophetic literature between divine judgment and husbands battering their wives is haunting and telling. It suggests that as far back as the days of biblical writings women in love were women in trouble. At the very least, it should convince those who dismiss feminist criticism of biblical language and biblical patriarchy as lacking depth, inconsequential, and trendy that there is probably more than a chance connection between patriarchy and violence against women.

Because most of their comments were directed against activities in the domain of cult and temple, the prophets aimed their messages at a male audience. Female sexual imagery ensured the prophets their audience's attention and a moral basis for evaluating the public activities of men in the cult and palace. Images of women in gaudy, seductive apparel, wives in hot pursuit of their lovers, and women with their skirts snatched up over their heads, exposing their private parts, became the stuff of moral and political reasoning as the prophets pondered, protested, and pontificated with other men in Hebrew society, accusing the women of loose behavior and warning them of a fate befitting whores.

This kind of imagery probably had a powerful effect on the prophets' predominantly male audience. The portrait of the sexually loose woman struck at the heart of two of the most cherished and sentimentalized institutions in Hebrew patriarchal culture: marriage and family. Ancient men were deeply invested in talk about wives deviating from the norms and wives flouting their marital responsibilities. After all, promiscuity in women posed a threat to social and property codes that were at the basis of Israel's patriarchal identity. This volume will show that the prophets' success or failure as orators depended in the end on their ability to convince their audiences that viable connections could be drawn between the norms governing the sexual behavior of women and God's demands on Israel.

It is virtually impossible to talk about women's sexuality in the Old Testament without also devoting attention to Hebrew marriage customs: sex and marriage went hand in hand. In fact, sex in ancient Israel was completely confined by law to marriage; any deviations, according to the law codes, bore fatal consequences for women and severe penalties for men. A woman's sexuality was the exclusive property of her husband or whatever man was the head of her household. Fathers were compensated for their daughters' compromised sexual status (Deut 22:28–29); brothers avenged their sisters' humiliation (e.g., Genesis 34; 2 Samuel 13); and, in the absence of close male kin, male cousins could broker the marriages of their female cousins (Esth 2:5ff.). Further, the narratives and legal materials amply attest to the dire consequences a man faced when he had sexual intercourse with a woman who was married to another man.[3] Intercourse with a married woman was menacing to a closed, endogamous society such as Israel for two reasons: first, it threatened to blur the ancestral and property lines that distinguished patriarchal households; second, it challenged a husband's status and honor within the community, calling into question his ability to control and protect the sexual impulses of the women in his household. As the prophets crafted their messages about the plight of their tiny nation, they cleverly exploited these widely held attitudes about the threat that wives posed to their husbands' prestige.

While in recent years there have been a number of interesting studies on the marriage metaphor, most of them have focused on the cultural and historical origins of the metaphor, tracing it back to its mythological origins in Ancient Near Eastern culture. These studies have seen in the marriage metaphor possible allusions to forbidden sexual and idolatrous practices. Only recently has sustained attention been paid to the metaphor's character as a literary device used to influence attitudes about marriage norms, gender roles, and power. Many recent works have been very helpful in increasing our understanding of not only the material significance of sex-related imagery but also the rhetorical effects of the imagery on the Hebrew literary imagination. It is my intention not to duplicate these studies but to build on them and to press further the interest in marriage as a literary trope for signifying cultural ideals.[4] In other words, our attention will be not on marriage and sexuality per se but on the activity of representing marriage and sexuality. Although marriage and sex are integral parts of the social vision of the Old Testament, considerable care was taken especially in Hebrew law to define when, with whom, and under what circumstances sex was permissible and when the boundaries of intimate relations might be undermined (see Leviticus 18). The marriage metaphor is important to this study insofar as it provides a frame for getting at the codes governing women's sexual behavior.

Perhaps more than any other material in the Bible, the portraits of women's sexuality drawn by Israel's prophets have contributed to the overall impression one gets from the Bible that women's sexuality is deviant, evil, and dangerous. This is so despite the fact that women, sex, and marriage were hardly of interest to prophets' overall messages, except as metaphors. At the center of the prophets' thinking was the political fate of the land, the history of the relationship between Israel and God, and an explanation for Israel's demise as a nation. Women, sex, and marriage were politicized in prophetic speeches and provided a means by which the prophets could integrate three separate but interrelated commentaries on Israelite society: the social world of Israel, the political fortunes of Israel, and the religious life of Israel. Despite the tendency of modern audiences to see marriage as a poetic device to fantasize about romance, courtship, and intimacy, for the prophets marriage was a trope for contemplating God's power and Israel's punishment.

This volume is, of course, the product of a larger, growing trend in biblical studies of examining the ways in which sexuality, politics, and the divine intersect. To see how these three topics cohere in a poetic metaphor about marriage requires an interdisciplinary approach to the Bible and an eclectic blend of methodological perspectives. I build on the insights of gender criticism, literary studies, studies of the erotic, and sociological and ideological analyses to illuminate the relationship between biblical literature and its social setting. Having said that, however, it is important to point out that this project is not a study of women's bodies and sexuality in biblical antiquity. That information is probably forever lost to us. Moreover, modern readers can grasp ancient ideas of women's bodies and female sexuality only as they have been re-presented and configured to us in cultural expressions.[5] In biblical antiquity, those expressions, as far as we can determine, were largely controlled by men.[6]

Drawing close connections between women's bodies and defilement, intimacy and power, violence and control, female nakedness and shame, dread and the erotic, the prophets were poets working within the conventions of ancient rhetoric and the rules of persuasion. They were cunning in their use of a metaphor that had the ability to evoke a range of powerful but contradictory responses in their audiences, and they were masterful in crafting imagery that was captivating and that generated new interpretations for centuries to come.

The first chapter of the book will situate the prophets' poetic constructions of marriage within the broader context of metaphorical speech in the Bible. This chapter draws on the work of linguists and philosophers of language to consider how metaphors work, how they rearrange reality by emphasizing some aspects of reality to the detriment of others, and how they lend themselves to various rhetorical agendas, especially those designed to arouse and sway audiences to a particular way of thinking. Among the many biblical metaphors used to symbolize the relationship of Israel and God, the image of marriage allowed the prophets to make some unique claims about the relationship of Israel and God and to draw some distinct conclusions about Israel's fate as a nation.

Because metaphors cannot be separated from the sociohistorical contexts that generate them and the sociohistorical contexts to which they seek to respond, the second chapter will reconstruct the ideological contexts inscribed in this rhetoric of dread and desire. Exploiting the cultural codes governing marriage to analogize divine–human relations did not originate with the prophets but was influenced by a broader mythological way of thinking that was common in the Ancient Near East. At that time, capital cities were understood as wives of the patron gods. The prophets skillfully built on and further manipulated this mythological representation of gender roles and women's sexuality for their own unique rhetorical purposes. Most important, regarding the attitudes about women assumed and reinforced by the imagery, we will question the assumptions about power, justice, and God that are expected of the audience, and the power structures within Israelite society that are criticized, challenged, and reconfigured by the prophets' use of the metaphor of marriage.

The third chapter shifts our attention away from the social dimensions of marital and sexual imagery to an exploration of what many agree is the real focus of biblical metaphors, namely, the insight they give us about God. It was ultimately God the prophets were attempting to talk about, and it was God the audiences continually failed to understand—or so the prophets thought. The metaphor of the promiscuous wife attempted to tell the prophets' audience something about God's ways, unique things about God that only marital and sexual imagery was capable of conveying—such things as the love of God, the honor of God, and the grace of God. We will see how a metaphor normally associated with romance, love, and sensuality is, in patriarchal thinking, transformed into a commentary on God's power. That is, the God who loves and rescues is the same God who destroys and abandons. According to the prophets, as a husband justly retaliates against his wayward, straying wife, so God justly terrorizes and destroys nations of people who fail to follow God's dictates.

The fourth and final chapter addresses the question invariably posed after any discussion of troubling biblical texts: What do we do with these texts? Is there any way to ignore them? Is it enough to say that they represent the prejudices and distorted views against women prevalent in their day and leave it at that? I do not pretend to offer comprehensive, totally satisfying answers to these and other questions about what to do with sacred texts that have counterliberation impulses and which, quite honestly, offend modern sensibilities. That matter remains a part of the unfinished agenda of liberation scholarship. I do think, however, that any discussion about such texts—and the metaphor of the promiscuous wife, as far as I am concerned, is one of them—must address the matter of the metaphor's effects on marginalized readers, especially those against whom it polemicizes. In short, what does it do to those who have been actually raped and battered, or who live daily with the threat of being raped and battered, to read sacred texts that justify rape and luxuriate obscenely in every detail of a woman's humiliation and battery? Moreover, what did it do to ancient Hebrew women to hear and be subjected to such ranting of prophets in the squares and marketplaces? The latter is a question that modern scholarship will probably never be able to answer. Nevertheless, it is still worthwhile, I think, for biblical scholars to consider the implications of our work and explore how different audiences respond(ed) to sexual imagery in prophetic speeches. We can do that by asking ourselves what parallels between an avenging male God and retaliating husbands convey to a female audience about masculinity, power, and justice? Conversely, what do parallels between an incorrigible nation and headstrong wives convey to a male audience about femininity, power, and justice?

Admittedly, my own interest in the metaphorical depictions of sexual violence in the Bible has had a lot to do with my identity as a woman—an African American woman. Undoubtedly, I have a lot to gain from demystifying biblical imagery that condones violence against socially marginalized women; but the fact that I am an African American and a female whose identity often evokes complicated, contradictory reactions within audiences, even theologically astute audiences, is not the only reason why the metaphor has for several years now preoccupied me. Other reasons why I continue to be fascinated with this metaphor have to do with its vision of hope, its utopian promises. The metaphor suggests that it is actually possible to recover love, romance, and intimacy in relationships that were once torn apart. The thought that it is possible to enter into, or to reenter, a relationship with God the creator that is as intimate and as satisfying as the best of any human relationships is almost impossible to resist. Even after we have decoded its stratagems, and despite its obscenity, the image of a woman and man triumphing in love after a season of battery and estrangement remàins a popular theme even in modern romance literature. We don't know where to begin to resist it. Do we simply dismiss its presence in the Bible, skip over it, or pretend it's not there?

The task for the ethically responsible exegete, it seems to me, is to help readers find ways to understand how literature both plays on our greatest fears and taps into our noblest ideals. We need to be able also to evaluate the way the metaphor of the promiscuous wife attempts to characterize what, in the prophets' minds, were very real oppressive impulses in Hebrew culture. For example, despite its obscene portrait of women, the metaphor of Israel as promiscuous wife represents an attempt by prophets to denounce malfeasance on the part of the ruling elite and to call attention to political greed, moral decay, religious syncretism, social disintegration, and egregious national policies. How do we affirm its positive side while simultaneously renouncing its negative effects?[7]

What do we do if the explanations that the prophets offer about evil, disaster, collective suffering, and global terror are unsatisfying? What do we do when metaphorical language ends up creating more problems than it solves? What happens when women refuse to accept any longer the blame for their physical battery by their husbands? What happens if they refuse any longer to believe that there are intelligent correlations between spousal abuse and God's redemption of the world?

All of our questions about biblical language will not be answered in this volume. Attending to one metaphor in the Bible, however odious, will not satisfy all our questions about women's oppression. What I attempt in the final pages of this study is to suggest ways modern readers might break the hold that terrifying texts have over the modern imagination—first by claiming our rights as readers to differ with authors, and, second, by deciding as readers, especially those marginalized by the texts, whether the worlds that authors place us in are indeed worth inhabiting.

As far as I am concerned, biblical metaphors are always worth reexamining. As often as society undergoes profound shifts in attitudes, and as one generation gives way to another, it is worth reexamining the metaphors we have inherited from the past to see to what extent, if at all, they remain relevant for talking about God and human existence.[8]

Finally, we have only to look around and examine the artifacts of our day—the headlines, billboards, commercials, advertisements, magazine covers, and the lyrics to our songs—to notice our own modern culture's fascination with sex and violence. The fact that women are much more likely to be the victims of sex and violent crimes than they are to be the perpetrators of such crimes must be kept in mind. Every three seconds somewhere around the world a woman is being beaten, and every three minutes somewhere a woman is being raped. If a book by a biblical scholar can help us examine the biblical basis for our distressing obsession with violence against women, then this project is imperative. In fact, if biblical scholarship is relevant to the way we live our lives today, if it has the potential to change the course of history, and if there are people who continue to read the Bible as a resource for modern living, then it is my responsibility as a woman and an African American to make certain that the scholarship I engage in as a biblical scholar does its part to work toward the larger project of critical, yet creative wrestling with biblical God-talk.

1

"You Have the Forehead of a Whore"
The Rhetoric of a Metaphor

The prophets of Israel went to extraordinary lengths to convey to their audiences the nature, extent, and consequences of their actions. The prophets repeatedly called upon some of the most explicit, provocative, and lurid images of human sexuality to personify what they saw as the nation's religious distortions and political blunders. Unforgettable scenes of the rape, abuse, and mutilation of women are detailed to symbolize what in the prophets' thinking was the disgraceful fate that awaited the nation. The prophet Hosea, for example, likened the northern capital city Samaria to a sexually depraved wife who, bent on chasing after lovers she sees as her benefactors, is doomed to be stripped naked, barricaded, and prevented by her husband from any further illicit contact with her lovers (Hos 2:1–13).[1] Two centuries later, after reminding the people that their devotion to God had been once like that of a bride to her new husband (Jer 2:1–3), the prophet Jeremiah compared Jerusalem's impending ruin to the humiliation a woman experiences when her skirt is snatched up over her head and her sexual parts are bared before the public (Jer 13:20–27). To the prophet Ezekiel's thinking, Jerusalem's recent ruin was like the downfall of a loose woman who, despite her husband's love, compassion, and lavish indulgences, had betrayed her husband's kindnesses, pursued lovers as dissolute as herself, and as a result rightly deserved to be left to the vilest impulses of her lovers (Ezekiel 16; 23). If this imagery is extravagant and explicit, it is supposed to be. After all, the prophets were poets. And how else do poets hope to arrest the attention of their audiences except by first seizing their imaginations?

At the basis of their repeated representations of Israel's social and political behavior as promiscuous, lewd, and shameless was the prophets' view that Israel had betrayed the terms of the covenant that her ancestors had entered into with God centuries earlier in the wilderness. There in the wilderness Israel had pledged her faithfulness to the terms of the covenant and her exclusive devotion to the one God Yahweh. It was the prophet Hosea who centuries later would construe that binding event as something like a marriage between a man and a woman. Israel and Yahweh had bound themselves to one another with mutual responsibilities and mutual understandings. Israel's failure to live up to the obligations and expectations of that bond was tantamount to marital infidelity and was legitimate cause for outrage and retaliation by her husband. Casting the divine–human relationship as a marriage relationship would prove—as we will see in this study—daring and provocative. The enduring benefit of convincing audiences to see the relationship between Israel and God as a marriage was that the prophets could exploit what was sure to be a range of widely held, deeply felt attitudes about marriage to shape their audiences' thinking about God's claim upon Israel. What better way of personifying that claim than by using as an analogy a human relationship where issues of power, propriety, property, and purity were profoundly at stake? What better strategy for rationalizing the just nature of God's punishment of Israel than by drawing parallels with a relationship where trust and fidelity were the basis of the relationship and where the dominant partner had the right and power to discipline and punish the subordinate one when the terms of the relationship have been breached? Furthermore, what better way to persuade their audiences to amend their ways than by drawing on an analogy that had the power to evoke strong feelings of shame and remorse?

Lurid, provocative descriptions of infidelity, depravity, and rape were intended to cast Israel's behavior in the strongest moral terms possible. Talking about the nation's history in provocative terms made their arguments compelling and unassailable. After all, each prophet's ministry spanned some of the most turbulent times in Israel's history, times of intrigue and disaster, times when, no doubt, conflicting views and interpretations of the events of the day were constantly exchanged in the temple, palace, square, and marketplace. The prophets found themselves faced with having to find an angle on the nation's future that guaranteed them a hearing.[2]

What we have in the prophets' use of marriage and sexual imagery, however, is not simply a matter of the prophets rendering in highly whimsical ways what could have been conveyed less dramatically. Undoubtedly, the prophets crafted their speeches in ways that were in all likelihood fully in keeping with the dominant conventions of Hebrew rhetoric. By characterizing Israel's relationship with its god as tantamount to the bond between a wife and a husband, and then depicting Israel's demise as like that of an adulterous wife who rightly—according to the mores of ancient society—must be punished, the prophets chose an image that had enormous sentimental value in Hebrew society. Its sentimental hold upon the population was sure to provide the prophets with audiences who had a moral and social stake in what the prophets had to say. After all, marriage and family norms were central to maintaining and perpetuating Israel's patriarchal culture, and dismantling the marriage relationship, as surely a wife's adultery threatened to do, posed a threat to every patriarchal household.[3] For that reason the marriage metaphor is sure to have been a very valuable tool for the prophets' rhetorical aims. Thus, like all prophets who competed for a hearing in public squares, Hosea, Jeremiah, and Ezekiel attempted to find an angle of vision that could tap into the most cherished interests and values of their audience—an angle that would have the power to stop an audience in their tracks.

Moreover, it seems evident that the prophets were also aware of the enormous power that descriptions of marriage and sexual behavior have over the imagination. When marriage, sex, and violence are framed in religious discussions in ways that draw connections between God and marriage, or God and sex, or God and violence, the discussion is tantalizing. Hence, Israel's prophets were not simply demagogues; they were chiefly rhetorists and poets. They understood, first, the power of figurative speech over the human imagination; and they understood, second, the power of that same speech to convey certain things about reality that no amount of paraphrase could impart. The marriage metaphor can be placed within the broader context of biblical metaphorical thinking as one of a number of poetic images on which the prophets drew in their never-ending quest to arrest and influence the thinking of their audiences.

Biblical Metaphors as Representations of Hebrew Reality

Because they were frequently trying to talk about themes that defy easy definition—love, peace, hope, suffering, death, faith, and the rest—Israel's prophets frequently found themselves relying on figurative language to convey what they wanted to say. In fact, the prophets used numerous tropes to help them traverse and talk about the vast and baffling nature of human existence, most especially the human and divine encounter. Since God was understood as both present and yet elusive, known but inscrutable, just and yet ambiguous, the most accessible language for talking about the divine, and in particular the relationship between the divine and humankind, was language borrowed from the realm of human relationships. In fact, human language was all the prophets had with which to talk about the God of Israel.[4]

The prophets Hosea, Jeremiah, and Ezekiel were not unique in their reliance on metaphors to talk about God and life. Metaphors have always been central to human expression. The Old Testament well attests to the centrality of metaphors in ancient Hebrew thinking: From God's self-assertion, "You have seen . . . how I bore you on eagles' wings and brought you to myself" (Exod 19:4), and the unnamed Philistine's rebuff to David, "Am I a dog that you come to me with sticks?" (1 Sam 17:43), to the Psalmist's outcry, "As a deer longs for flowing streams, so my soul longs for you, O God" (Ps 42:1), and Nahum's condemnation of Nineveh, "Your guards are like grasshoppers, your scribes like swarms of locusts settling on the fences on a cold day" (Nah 3:17). The Israelites' thinking about the divine and human existence was expressed by drawing on analogies from everyday life.[5] Five human relationships are used as metaphors repeatedly in prophetic speeches to describe the relationship between Israel and Yahweh: (1) judge and litigant, (2) parent and child, (3) master and slave, (4) king and vassal, and (5) husband and wife.[6] Thus, the prophets were dependent on their own social institutions to describe their experiences of the divine. Only by using the "this" of their own cultural universe—namely, the everyday institutional life of first-millennium Palestine—were they able to talk about the "That" which they understood as standing above their universe, namely, Yahweh their god. Thus, we discover that God, like human beings, sees and hears, commands and repents, judges and forgives, punishes and rewards, pleads with and castigates, loves and hates, and is jealous and commits rape. The prophets drew on their own mortal experiences of relationships in order to explain what it meant to be devoted to God.

The theologian Sallie McFague has described perhaps most concisely and eloquently what metaphorical thinking involves:

"Thinking metaphorically means spotting a thread of similarity between two dissimilar objects, events, or whatever, one of which is better known than the other, and using the better known one as a way of speaking about the lesser known."[7] The Hebrew prophets, in their never-ending quest to illumine the character of God's claim on Israel, offered a variety of lenses/ metaphors through which their audiences might view that claim. In each instance the prophets perceived some "thread of similarity" between established patterns of human interchange (e.g., marriage, parenting, slavery, imperial status, and legal standing) and the relationship between Israel and God.

By appealing again and again to these five metaphors, the prophets would enforce and reinforce for their hearers a number of important precepts about the divine–human bond. First, the prophets insisted that the bond between God and Israel was that of a relationship. In fact, all five metaphors taken together insist that God can be known only through an intimate, meaningful relationship, not through abstract contemplation devoid of commitment. Second, the prophets maintained that the relationship between deity and people was not an egalitarian one but was one of hierarchy and authority. In other words, God and Israel were not equals. Indeed, parallels existed between God's rights over Israel and a superior's rights over a subordinate, and those rights were non-negotiable and firmly established (e.g., parent and child, master and slave). Third, the prophets argued in their use of these five metaphors that the relationship between God and Israel was marked by mutual obligations and mutual responsibilities, that both parties had tasks and responsibilities appropriate to their roles in the relationship, but that the burden of the relationship rested firmly on the shoulders of the subordinate partner. It was the latter's task to conform not only to the stated rules of the relationship but also to live up to the unspoken expectations that framed the relationship. In fact, it was important for the subordinate not to do anything that might be interpreted as an act of insubordination or of disrespect to the superior: the vassal must pay homage to the king; the slave must be subservient to the master; the wife must show honor to her husband. Fourth, and finally, each prophet insisted that failure by the subordinate to fulfill her or his responsibility virtually guaranteed punishment, retribution, or discipline (depending on the metaphor): judges punished defendants; kings banished or executed servants; masters beat slaves; parents disciplined children; and husbands divorced or assaulted wives.

Metaphors of Power and Punishment

From these four recurring precepts of Hebrew metaphorical thinking one can sum up the prophets' poetic imagery as "metaphors of power and punishment."[8] Each metaphor emphasized that the divine–human relationship operated within a frame of fixed rules of behavior and expectations, rules that in various ways perpetuated a system of relating that stressed hierarchy, domination, and retribution, rules that gave the dominant partner the right to penalize or retaliate against the subordinate should rules be broken, expectations be unmet, or warnings go unheeded. In this poetic world of fixed power relations, it is not surprising that God was always masculinized as the husband and Israel was always feminized as the wife. The power issues in the metaphor did not tolerate any diversion from these gender-based roles.

However asymmetrical may have been the power in the relationship between dominant and subordinate partner, at the basis of metaphors of power and punishment was the claim that with the relationship between God and Israel came mutual duties and mutual understandings. For example, just as a husband entered into a relationship with his wife promising to provide her material and physical security, so did a wife enter that relationship with pledges and promises. In exchange for her husband's provisions and protection, she presumably pledged her sexual loyalty and emotional faithfulness. Hence, the husband figure in the speeches of Hosea, Jeremiah, and Ezekiel clearly had the upper hand in the marriage (his wife's sexuality, loyalty, and her very body belonged to him; her fate rested in his hands). Despite the power that the husband had over the wife in the relationship, however, prophetic speeches centered repeatedly not on the husband's obligations but on the wife's obligations. It was her actions (or, rather, her failure to live up to her obligations) that consistently dominates the metaphor's attention in all the speeches of the prophets.

In the prophetic descriptions, the husband repeatedly reminds his wife that he has fulfilled his side of the relationship—he has fed, clothed, and protected her (Hos 2:8; Ezek 16:1–8). It is the wife's failures and indiscretions that are repeatedly elaborated upon: her false claims about her lover (Hos 2:5, 12), her sexually extravagant and wanton behavior (Ezek 16:15–22), her flagrant failure to remain faithful to her husband (Jer 3:3, 10; 4:30; Ezek 16:33–34). The husband threatens to punish and/or divorce his wife. She has repeatedly failed to live up to her side of the relationship (Jer 13:25–27; Hos 2:8–13; Ezek 16:25–52; 23).[9] The implication is clear: the wife deserves to be punished. The point of the marriage metaphor, like the other four metaphors, is to justify the violence and punishment the subordinate endures and to exonerate the dominant partner from any appearance of being unjust.

God, then, is not a harsh, cruel, vindictive husband who threatens and beats his wife simply because he has the power to do so. He is himself a victim, because he has been driven to extreme measures by a wife who has again and again dishonored him and has disregarded the norms governing marriage relations. Likewise, God is not a capricious authority figure who deliberates as a cold and distant potentate; according to the king metaphor, God sovereignly administers the affairs of Israel, always with Israel's best interests at heart (Psalms 47, 89, 99,

145). Nor is God the judge who is heartless, merciless, and detached from God's judgments (Psalms 9, 10, 82); instead, God's mercy, say the prophets, has proved to be everlasting. Similarly, God as parent is not a detached authoritarian figure who, like a despot, metes out punishment unsparingly; rather, like every parent, God laments and anguishes over the prospect of disciplining a dearly beloved child (Hos 11:8–9). The point emphasized by all five metaphors of power and punishment, therefore, is that whereas God's power over Israel may be absolute, God's motivations for punishing Israel are never arbitrary or heartless.

Although prophetic metaphors stress hierarchy, domination, and retribution in the divine–human bond—concepts that in our modern context warrant considerable scrutiny—it is important to hear these metaphors with the ears of a tiny kingdom. To a vulnerable, powerless, imperiled nation such as ancient Israel, each metaphor would have been reassuring, for each insisted in its own way that, despite a nation's subordinate status, it could still enjoy protection, security, and a modicum of fame.[10] Each metaphor promoted the idea that it was possible for a tiny nation to experience order, peace, stability, and justice amid threatening surroundings. Each insisted that, even though small and subordinate, Israel enjoyed a special, unique claim to its relationship with God. And the only condition for its permanent safety and protection was the nation's obedience. The key was to pattern one's behavior toward the omnipotent, omniscient creator of the earth after the model of human relationships between dominant and subordinate parties. One partner is loyal, devoted, totally dependent on the other partner for protection and sustenance. Failure to behave according to this hierarchy had its own natural consequences: the weaker partner risked being punished and chastised by the stronger partner.

Thus, the metaphors of the prophets invited listeners to consider parallels between the way God responded and related to Israel and the way humans responded and related to one another. God's authority over Israel, therefore, was seen as not just palpable but natural. Similarly, God's demands upon Israel were not simply comprehensible; they were reasonable. For example, according to the parent–child metaphor,[11] like a parent, God could not easily dismiss God's responsibility to care for and protect God's children (Israel), even though, Israel, like children, frequently rebelled against the parent's authority and provoked the parent to chastise and discipline the child. Nevertheless, according to the imagery of the prophets, when God did condemn Israel to punishment, God was acting well within God's duties as a parent.

Metaphors of power and punishment not only capture the basis of social relations; they naturalize the ideological framework of those relationships. They do this by rendering the power structures and dynamics in those relationships virtually inviolable. Once again we can take the example of the parent–child metaphor. Of the five metaphors, this one might arguably be the most intransigent. It has endured because the power dynamics between parents and children have remained virtually constant and instinctive across the centuries. So widely recognized are parents' power and rights over their children that it is only within the last half century, and only in a handful of countries, that the notion of children's rights has begun to emerge. Indeed, so esteemed were parents in Hebrew culture that honoring them was a divine command (Exod 20:12), presumably on the grounds that they, like God, create and mold life. An unruly child who failed to obey and show respect to his or her parents could be stoned to death (Deut 21:18–21). Parents' rights to discipline and correct their children were taken for granted; after all, who could know better the purpose and identity of the being created than its creator, who shapes and corrects in whatever way the creator sees fit (e.g., Jer 18:1–4; Isa 45:9–13)?

Another important assumption of the parent–child metaphor

was that children were somehow the *property* of their parents. Children were considered to belong to their parent in ways that differed from a husband's claim upon his wife's sexuality. The bond between parent and child was viewed as inherent and indissoluble. Parents could exercise power over their child's life like the power that God the Father-Mother exercised over Israel —not simply because of the rights granted to parents by the legal system but because of the incredible emotional attachment parents have to their children. It is in this regard that one might speak of a child being the property of its parents—not merely in the material or bodily sense but in the sense of the emotional bond the parent has to the child. Thus, the parent–child metaphor, like the husband–wife metaphor, was capable of stressing the tremendous emotional tug-of-war that lay just beneath the surface of the divine–human drama.[12]

What will become evident throughout this study are the ways in which the marriage metaphor reinforced certain attitudes about power and punishment in divine–human roles and, in collaboration with the other popular biblical metaphors, helped to create an interlocking system of imagery that interpreted and influenced how audiences understood God and their relationship to God. As one of a number of metaphors the prophets appealed to in order to make sense of the world as their audiences knew it, the marriage metaphor only confirmed what were already established dynamics of life (e.g., power, domination, hierarchy, dualism) and images of God (e.g., powerful, dominating, punitive). Metaphors became central to prophetic rhetoric because prophets were frequently trying to communicate about the more intangible aspects of divine–human reality (e.g., love, joy, peace, faith) in ways that were familiar, intelligible, and natural to their audiences. But before considering metaphors as rhetorical devices, we will need to consider see how metaphors shape our thinking and our reality.

How Metaphors Work

Max Black, a literary critic, offers a helpful illustration of how metaphors work. He takes a simple figurative expression, such as "Israel is a luxuriant vine" (Hos 10:1) and refers to the two subjects in this sentence as the principal one ("Israel") and the subsidiary one ("vine").[13] In the mind of the audience, says Black, a set of attributes commonly associated with vines (e.g., pretentious, stubborn, wild, excessive) is conjured up, which he calls "associated commonplaces." Hearing Israel associated with a vine, audiences are inclined to transfer a number of cultural stereotypes ("associated commonplaces") to the principal subject. Once the connection between Israel and vines is made, Israel begins to be understood by audiences as pretentious, stubborn, wild, and excessive; and all of Israel's behavior and history begin to take on new meaning. But attributes are not the only things that are associated with Israel when the metaphor vine is evoked. The (set of) *attitudes* that listeners have toward vines (e.g., annoyance, frustration, impatience) is also transferred to Israel. In that way, attributes and attitudes combine to determine not simply how one is to understand Israel but, most significantly, how one is expected to react to or feel about Israel.

What makes metaphorical speech especially effective as a form of social rhetoric is precisely its ability to reorganize our way of thinking about—and reacting to—the subsidiary subject in new and different ways, drawing connections between the two subjects where connections had not been seen before, calling attention to some attributes and not others, and deliberately rousing certain kinds of emotional responses in an audience. In short, metaphors play upon cultural stereotypes; they stress some attributes while deliberately ignoring others. In the statement "Israel is a vine," only the characteristics in Israel that are most like a vine are accentuated; those completely unlike a vine are not part of the picture. Israel is stubborn according to the metaphor of the vine, but this image does not account for the description of Israel's history with God as one also marked by fickleness and shame, which are not attributes associated with vines. To represent these attributes and to present a fuller picture of the diversity of human experience, other metaphors are needed.

Thus, metaphors do not have to give accurate portraits of reality in order to be effective. Audiences do not have to recognize in the vine metaphor an accurate depiction of what vines are actually like; nor do they have to recognize in the marriage metaphor a thorough or complete representation of what Israel was like. The audience only has to perceive a "thread of similarity" between the two subjects in order for the metaphor to be a competent signifier.[14] But those metaphors that wind up finally as memorable and enduring in audiences' minds are the ones that tap into widely held, deeply felt values or attitudes within an audience. In other words, audiences must *care* about the social picture the metaphor is capturing. Hence, a metaphor about marriage tends to have more lasting value than a metaphor about vines because people tend to be more emotionally and socially invested in their intimate relationships with each other than they are in the quality and care of vines from year to year.[15]

This does not mean that analogies to vines are of no value. A statement such as "Israel is a vine" is able to picture Israel as uncontrollable and pretentious in a way that no other metaphor can. In the same way, the image "Israel is a promiscuous wife" emphasizes attributes of Israel and invites reactions to Israel that other metaphors do not. The image of Israel as vine could make listeners feel the divine disappointment of God with the people who were guilty of unconstrained entanglements with idols and displays of false piety (Hos 10:1). Despite its unique ability to signify Israel as out of control, the vine metaphor was totally incapable of calling to mind the image of Israel as also lewd and depraved. To convince their audiences that their behavior not only disappointed God but also dishonored and humiliated

God, the prophets found themselves having to rely on the marriage metaphor to traverse the complex world of Mediterranean shame and honor codes.

Returning once more to Black's explanation of how metaphors work, we are pointed to the indeterminant character of metaphors. According to Black, it is impossible to determine how different audiences will perceive the interaction between principal and subsidiary subjects, since a metaphor's meaning and effect can differ with context. That is because the associated commonplaces, or stereotypes, are culturally determined and can differ from one generation to another, from one culture to another, or from one reader to another. Metaphors, therefore, are not timelessly applicable to every context nor timelessly relevant to every generation; the values, assumptions, and worldview inherent in a metaphor can differ according to context. We will see just how true this is when we raise the question in the last chapter about whether the marriage metaphor, which relies on a contrivance of gender roles for its stability, continues to be a meaningful device for imaging divine–human relations for the modern context.

Marriage as a Controlling Metaphor

In the end, a metaphor's success depends on its ability to bring two separate objects into cognitive and emotional relation in such a way that "it becomes virtually impossible to view the lesser known one without referring to the better known one."[16] That being the case, it is virtually impossible to think of the God of Israel in the Bible as anything other than male (husband) and the people of Israel as anything other than female (wife). These stereotypes have influenced generations of religious imagining about God and Israel. It is precisely this enduring ability to bring a range of behaviors and attitudes associated with gender to bear upon divine–human relations that makes the marriage metaphor what Terence Fretheim in his study of images of God calls a "controlling metaphor."[17] By that Fretheim means that the marriage metaphor brings together for an audience language and activity from the unconscious level that effectively give coherence to biblical thinking about God. Thus, when God and Israel were construed metaphorically as husband and wife, a gamut of images associated with the drama of such a relationship emerged out of the controlling metaphor. A whole range of behavior associated with intimacy and mating was brought to mind.

For example, the earliest days of God and Israel's relationship were cast as the period of courtship; the covenant in the wilderness became a marriage; Israel's idolatry was interpreted as betrayal and adultery; Israel's estrangement was divorce; and the reunion of God and Israel was reconciliation. Upon hearing God and Israel cast as husband and wife, then, audiences were able to draw on their experiences of the stages of male and female bonding to bring coherence to and to shed light on their knowledge of God and Israel's erratic history together. Whereas the forensic metaphor invited the audience to trace God and Israel's relationship through the observable stages of the judicial process (violation, summons, verdict, and pardon) and the parent–child metaphor pictured the normal stages from birth to maturity, the marriage metaphor had the potential to bring coherence to a host of unstated assumptions and imperceptible rules that shaped behavior, attitudes, and reactions, which communities share and by which they governed themselves. Moreover, the subplots of love, sex, and jealousy, which the marriage metaphor invariably propels upon the divine–human drama, introduced an element of unpredictability to the affairs of God and Israel that other metaphors could not paraphrase. God and Israel's relations were marked by emotional high and low periods; not all expectations were explicit, as much of male and female dealings with one another could be downright irrational. As a controlling metaphor, therefore, the marriage metaphor has the symbolic potential to illuminate a range of behavior the prophets saw as characteristic of, but more specifically as idiosyncratic to, Israel's history with God.

Finally, the strength of the marriage metaphor as a controlling metaphor was its ability to leave some elements of the divine–human realm to the realm of the unpredictable. While Israel acted completely like the depraved wife, God as husband was not so easily cast. God as betrayed husband expressed a range of human emotions that could make God seem as erratic as Israel. For example, prophet after prophet drew on a wide spectrum of sexual activities—from marriage (covenant), to infidelity (apostasy), to sexual violence (punishment/judgment), to sexual reunion (covenant renewal)—to describe the vicissitudes of Israel and God's history together.[18] Their history had taken unexpected turns, in part because, like an unfaithful wife, Israel had failed to conduct herself in accordance with the mores and expectations that governed married women. That same history had also taken unexpected turns because God sometimes failed to respond to Israel's infidelities in predictable ways. God was forgiving when one would expect God, like any honorable male, to be unforgiving. Even though outside liaisons were forbidden, unthinkable, dangerous, and disgraceful, Israel repeatedly dishonored her husband by acting shamefully with other men. And when her debauchery and depravity should have spelled her death (Lev 20:10; cf. Deut 22:25–27), Israel was unexpectedly spared, insisted each propher. Instead of killing or divorcing his wife (as he surely would have been expected to do) God unexplainably welcomed back his incorrigible wife with the invitation to begin anew.[19] Casting Israel's history with Yahweh in a marriage drama allowed the prophets to play upon the unpredictability of love and romance.

Male Prestige in the Marriage Metaphor

Although Hosea was the first to develop fully in the Hebrew Bible the metaphor of the covenant as a conjugal bond between

Israel and God, the marriage metaphor itself probably did not originate with this prophet. It was probably derived from the Ancient Near Eastern custom of personifying the land, the nation, and capital cities as female figures.[20] According to this imagery, as far back as the time of the wilderness, when the nation was like a pubescent virgin, Israel had sworn herself in covenant loyalty to her husband, the one God.

> I remember the devotion of your youth,
>   your love as a bride,
> how you followed me in the wilderness,
>   in a land not sown.
> Israel was holy to the LORD,
>   the first fruits of the LORD's harvest.
> All who ate of it were held guilty;
>   disaster came upon them,
>   says the Lord.
>   (Jer 2:2b–3)

But as time passed, Israel, according to this metaphor, turned out to be the quintessentially depraved wife. Hers was a history of flagrantly violating the founding premise of patriarchy—namely, that a woman's sexuality did not belong to her but was the property of the men in her family.

By brazenly, persistently, and wantonly pursuing other lovers, Israel had defied the social order, violated her relationship with her husband, betrayed his trust, rebelled against his authority, and, above all, had shamed her husband by defiling her body (that is, her husband's property) through sexual involvements with other men. Each prophet would use the metaphor to denounce Israel's social, political, and religious practices and to rationalize Israel's impending destruction. The prophets would portray God not as an impartial judge, or as a disappointed parent, but as a deeply passionate, rightly offended husband who responded as he did because he had been betrayed. The advantage of the marriage metaphor in casting Israel as a woman was its ability to construe Israel's behavior not simply as rebellion or immaturity but as depravity and shamelessness. Likewise, through the marriage metaphor God's reaction became all the more legitimate because he was acting not merely as a disappointed parent but as an enraged and dishonored man. The metaphor of the promiscuous wife expected its audience to share the values and attitudes of Hebrew society—the belief in a wife's exclusive sexual devotion to her husband, her failure to do so constituting shame on her part that brought dishonor upon her husband and warranted retaliation. The prophets expected their audiences to share these fundamental understandings. Otherwise, the metaphor would have made no sense to them.

Of the five metaphors that reappear in the prophets, only the marriage metaphor was capable of signifying failure to obey and conform to the prevailing norms as a moral and social disgrace. Neither a child's defiance, nor a defendant's violation, nor the vassal and servant's disobedience inherently connoted shame. Only sexual promiscuity within marriage could capture this fully. That is because the image of the promiscuous wife played upon a range of ideas that tapped into some of the deepest, most subliminal social codes within a culture. Marriage forced audiences to confront their attitudes and assumptions about human sexuality in general, and women's sexuality in particular, in ways that none of the other biblical metaphors was capable of doing. It also called upon audiences to reaffirm their belief in a male honor system where a man's prestige rested in great part on his ability to control the behavior of the subordinates in his household (e.g., wives, slaves, children). Even though all five metaphors insisted that the power relations between God and Israel were not equal, and that ultimately God had the power to retaliate against Israel when Israel failed to meet its obligations, only the marriage metaphor could uniquely claim that failure to obey brought shame upon the dominant partner and eventually upon the subordinate one.

Marriage, Sexuality, and the Female Body

Both the female body and female sexuality proved to be ideal vehicles, on the one hand, for connoting the shame and humiliation that resulted from Israel's actions, and, on the other hand, for tapping into the enormous passion and sentimentality tied up with God's claim on Israel. The stereotypical belief that the female body and female sexuality were somehow dangerous, disgusting, threatening, and needing to be controlled played well into the prophets' efforts to push their audiences to perceive both the abnormality of their behavior and the perils that lay ahead should they continue on their course. It should come as no surprise, therefore, that throughout the prophets' writings the marriage metaphor is used almost exclusively to personify Israel negatively and to paint its history with God as volatile. In this way, the woman in the marriage metaphor stands in sharp ideological contrast to the woman in the parent–child metaphor: whereas in the former she was shameless, depraved, unfaithful, and gullible, in the latter she was devoted, compassionate, loving, and nurturing. Not surprisingly, the woman in the marriage metaphor is always Israel, whereas in the parent metaphor God can be male or female.[21] We find in these two metaphors contradictory constructions of womanhood. In real life, Hebrew women undoubtedly made important contributions to their society as mothers and wives, but in the hands of Israel's poets and demagogues, women as mothers were idealized and women as wives were problematized.[22] In both roles women were sexual beings, but their sexuality posed serious threats to society if it was not in the service of procreating legitimate heirs for their husbands.

It is important to point out that symbolizing Israel's fortunes and fate with images taken from the experiences of women was not an effort on the prophets' part to challenge, supplant, or compensate for the overwhelming masculine imagery (e.g., son, king, warrior) used throughout the Bible to symbolize God and Israel. Metaphors from the public and private worlds of andro-centric activities were firmly established in patriarchal biblical thinking. With the marriage metaphor, however, the prophets "perceived a thread of similarity" between the unique roles and experiences of ancient Israelite women and certain deplorable aspects of Israel's behavior. They perceived parallels between the measures husbands took to chastise wives and the measures God took to correct Israel. They signified Israel's disgrace and reproach by drawing parallels with the horror and shame attached to women who committed adultery and women who were ritually impure. Indeed, the experiences of married women allowed the prophets to organize Israel's history along the lines of women's sexual life cycles (e.g., marriage, menstruation, child-birth, widowhood) and according to the strict mores governing their sexual appetite (adultery and fornication). It follows, then, that the three major recurring motifs of the female-identified metaphors found in the prophetic writings are marriage/adul-tery, giving birth, and prostitution.[23]

On the matter of the unique bond that exists between God and Israel, the marriage metaphor (like the parent–child metaphor) conveyed the notion that the covenant relationship between God and Israel created a quasi-familial bond between the two where love and trust undergirded the relationship. But at times the love was a menacing sort, one that drove a husband (God) to plead, cajole, stalk, and threaten his wife (Israel). In this image, divine love was as uncompromising and jealous as it was compassion-ate and tender.[24] The husband's love was fueled by some very definite notions about the rights and privileges of the husband. Having as he did the power to divorce his wife, the authority to haul her before the cult on charges of infidelity, and the right to his wife's exclusive sexuality, the husband clearly had the upper hand in the relationship. In fact, the metaphor is comprehensible only if one concedes that indeed the husband was fully within his rights to retaliate physically against his wife for her offenses against him.

But metaphors can also shock us with their reversals. They do not simply nor always imitate real life. They sometimes, for effect, deviate from reality and from our expectations. As we have already seen, although God, according to the metaphor, was within God's right to destroy Israel fully or to banish Israel forever for the nation's idolatry, in the end, according to all three prophets, God stood ready to be reconciled with God's servant, child, or bride Israel. Obviously, in each instance God's forgiveness would prove to be as shocking to the prophets' audiences as Israel's depravity was sure to have been. The betrayed husband forgave his depraved wife, proving himself to be the superior one in the relationship. Not only did he have social and economic power over his wife; he was also morally superior to her in that he forgave her when it was fully within his rights and power to have her stoned to death.

Finally, the prophets saw in Hebrew men's fear of women's sexuality and bodily functions just the sort of anxiety and fears that would allow the metaphor of the promiscuous wife to convey the danger and threat that the prophets believed certain contemptible religious and social practices symbolized for Israel. Sexual imagery proved especially suitable to express the inevitability of the chaos and dishonor that were sure to descend upon Israel, just as chaos and dishonor would follow socially if one's wife failed to conduct herself properly.[25]

In the hands of Israel's poets, the marriage metaphor was not simply one of a number of metaphors innocently representing one of a number of unique aspects of divine–human relations. Instead, the marriage metaphor, with its unavoidable commentary on appropriate and inappropriate behavior for wives, permitted audiences in ancient Israelite circles to contemplate the repulsive, dishonorable side of their religious, social, and political history. The metaphor was not interested, as some have supposed, in stressing romance, intimacy, and mutuality. Rather, the metaphor focused on belittling female judgment and condemning the wife as fickle, untrustworthy, loose, and stubborn. At the same time, the metaphor elevated the husband to the position of noble benefactor, innocent of any semblance of wrongdoing. Compared to the other four recurring metaphors, then, only the marriage metaphor lifted God's retaliations out of the realm of senseless violence and made sure that God's pardon would not be viewed as weakness on God's part. According to this metaphor in particular, in the world of love and intimacy—and given all the complexities that sex and sexuality introduce into relationships —the heart is not only unpredictable. It is downright irrational.

Conclusion

Metaphorical language is at the center of how ancient prophets conceived of and understood the world, themselves, and God. Whether relationships were personified as like that of shepherd and sheep, judge and defendant/plaintiff, king and vassal, master and slave, father and son, or husband and wife, the task was to impress upon one's audience that God can be known only through an intimate, meaningful relationship, and not through abstract contemplation devoid of commitment. Metaphors such as parent–child and more specifically the marriage metaphor envisioned a relationship that was quasi-familial. More specifically, each of the popular metaphors of the day asserted in its own way (1) that the relationship between God and humankind was a relation of unequals; (2) that that relationship was one of mutual expectations and responsibility; (3) that the burden of the relationship fell upon the subordinate partner, whose responsibility it was not to offend or bring dishonor upon the dominant patron;

and (4) that God, as the dominant partner in the relationship, had the power to punish and direct the relationship in ways that ensured the relationship's conformity to social standards.

But metaphors are products of human speech, and speech in order to be effective and capable of being understood takes place within concrete social contexts. Metaphors originate in social contexts and reinforce social contexts. This means, then, that in order to grasp how the marriage metaphor impacts a culture, one must situate the metaphor of the promiscuous wife, for example, within its social, institutional, and historical context. Audiences accept, reject, esteem, and forget metaphors in proportion to the metaphors' ability or inability to square with a web of emotional, social, political, historical, institutional data. We now turn to the matter of examining the social systems and contexts of audiences that, upon hearing God described as a raging, betrayed husband who batters and humiliates his promiscuous wife (Israel) into subjection, would perceive some similarities with their reality.

2

"Is She Not My Wife?" Prophets, Audiences, and Expectations

Speakers make demands on their audiences. They demand that their audiences share their vision of the way things ought to be and agree with them about how to bring about such a vision. Audiences who don't agree or haven't made up their minds yet whether they agree with speakers but who are willing to hear them out are asked to *pretend* that they do agree until they've had a chance to experience the full logic of the speaker's argument. Temporarily suspending one's own opinions until one has had the opportunity to hear a speaker out is important in communication. To experience the Hebrew prophets' use of marital and sexual imagery is to be prepared to suspend one's own opinions about marriage and sexuality long enough to evaluate the prophets' message. But suspending one's opinion is not all one must do. To experience the prophets' language, to follow their logic, and to hear the prophets out, one must be willing to share the value systems the prophets operate within, see the world through their eyes, stand in their shoes—or pretend to do so. It is a strategy for communication that is aptly summed up by the expression "for the sake of argument."

One may in the end roundly reject the prophets' argument, of course, but to do that one must first hear the argument out. As any rhetorist would, the prophets of Israel crafted their speeches fully expecting to be heard out. They were smart enough to know that their messages would not be received by everyone,[1] but neither did they expect their messages to be rejected by everyone. The aim of this chapter is to explore how the prophets structured their arguments to anticipate the attitudes and assumptions of their audiences. We are interested in the way the prophets used marriage and sexual imagery to communicate with audiences in concrete social situations that shaped their worldviews and their values. How did the prophets use the marriage metaphor to win their audiences' attention? How did they use body imagery and gender roles to make themselves understood by those who shared their views about women, about men, about marriage, and about human sexuality? How did they shape their rhetoric to get through to those who were inclined to hear them out?

When we raise questions about the audiences and their social worlds, we are confronted with a number of challenges. First, any audience we try to reconstruct is one we recreate in large part with our imaginations. The audience(s) whose culture, languages, customs, worldviews, and religion lay behind the biblical texts have long ceased to exist. We do not share the myth, the heritage, and the worldview of the audiences of the Old Testament prophets. Thus, while the object of this chapter is to explore the cluster of cultural attitudes that the rhetoric of sex attempts to address, our understanding will be influenced in great part by *our* reactions to this rhetoric, *our* theories about rhetoric, *our* thinking about sex and power, *our* models for conceiving of the way the world operates, and *our* conventions for reading texts.

Second, in contrast to our colleagues who study early Christian texts, those of us specializing in the Old Testament do not have access to extrabiblical literature from the biblical period that theorizes about Hebrew rhetoric. For the student of Hebrew rhetoric there is nothing like Aristotle's *Poetics* or Cicero's *De*

Inventione or Quintilian's *Institutio Oratoria* to help us understand the social conventions that shaped the way Hebrew people
wrote or spoke. Nor do we have in the extant literature from
neighboring cultures stylistically similar literature with which
we can compare and contrast Hebrew conventions for writing
and speaking.[2] In short, we have neither within the Old Testament nor external to the Old Testament any explicit information
about the assumptions that underlie Hebrew rhetoric. Without
this kind of information, we are forced to rely on the literature of
the Old Testament to help illuminate principles behind Hebrew
rhetoric. We proceed in our endeavors, however, mindful that
rhetoric and literature are not the same thing, that sometimes
texts are written (and prophets speak) in ways that deliberately
deviate from conventional forms of communicating. In those
cases, the deviations are meant to signify meaning and to
become clues that audiences are expected to pick up on.[3] Thus,
although we lack the data to help us situate our observations of
prophetic rhetoric within the larger cultural practices of the
Hebrew world, nevertheless our interest is in the ways the
prophets used metaphors to signal meaning to their audiences,
to reinforce values in their audiences, and to build upon widely
held beliefs. This way we might better understand how prophets
communicated with and signaled to their audience how to hear
them out.

Third, there is the related problem of pinpointing exactly what
we mean by "audience" when we talk about the literature of the
Old Testament. How can we talk credibly about the ancient audiences to whom the prophets directed their messages when we
take into account the length of time between the prophets and
the preserving, compiling, and editing of what has come to be
regarded as the Old Testament? The prophets' messages under-
went centuries of transmission in some cases, both orally and in
writing. Each new social setting through which the prophetic
oracles passed may have given rise to reflection and editorial

revision. How is it possible, then, to speak of reconstructing the prophets' original audiences when the traditions passed through the hands of generations of audiences? Related to that, how is it possible to talk credibly about "prophets," given the clear influence of the Deuteronomic school on books such as Hosea and Jeremiah, and given the heavy Priestly influence on the book of Ezekiel?

The first two challenges are caveats that scholars of biblical literature continually confront whenever they presume to talk about the biblical past. Because the actual culture of the Old Testament is forever lost to us, and because we lack documents that would allow us to understand where prophetic rhetoric fits into the principles of Ancient Near Eastern elocution, our conclusions about the social world of biblical texts are admittedly speculative and are intended only to be thought provoking.

As for the matter of how to talk about "prophets" and "audiences," given the composite nature of these books, we should make clear some distinctions. First, there is a difference between the actual prophets who composed the speeches and the ideal prophets who are assumed in the speeches, as there are differences between the actual audiences who first encountered the prophets' messages and the ideal audiences anticipated in the construction of those messages.[4] Whenever the words "prophet" and "audience" are used in this book, it is the ideal prophet and the ideal audience that concern us—that is, the prophet and the audience presupposed by the way the speech is laid out. Each prophetic text, by virtue of the choices that went into structuring it and by the very crafting of the rhetoric, has its ideal author and its ideal audience. Even though we could never hope to recover the actual first receivers of the prophets' messages, we can deduce, from a study of the way imagery is constructed, something about the hypothetical audience(s) who would identify with the messages contained in these texts.[5]

Talk about prophets and audiences and the way the former

fashioned their messages according to the tastes, habits, and competencies of the latter, and the way both are configured and idealized in books named for prophets is indeed a fairly modern way of thinking about prophetic literature. Influenced by more than two decades of debate in modern literary circles about readers and texts, attention has shifted away from the autonomous status of the text to (1) the role readers play in determining the meaning of texts, (2) the way texts are shaped to anticipate their readers' worldview and to have certain effects upon their readers, and (3) the way in which texts affect different readers differently.[6] Many of these conclusions have begun to find their way into Old Testament studies, and new works are appearing regularly. Some studies have focused on the way subjects are constructed in biblical texts, while other works have examined the ways in which Old Testament texts are constructed to stabilize the interests of certain audiences and to destabilize the interests of others.[7]

Biblical scholars have always had a variety of methods available to help them find out about the cultural systems undergirding biblical documents. As early as a hundred years ago, Hermann Gunkel used the insights from literary criticism in his study of the forms of Hebrew literature. One important insight that has emerged in conjunction with cross-disciplinary scholarship is the notion that communication is a social convention. That is, communication is based on a whole network of codes having to do with mutual expectations, mutual assumptions, and mutual capabilities. Form criticism attempted to provide interpreters with skills necessary to explore the way in which some expectations become codified in conventional forms of speech (genres and traditions) and are transmitted through institutional settings (their *Sitz im Leben,* or "setting in life"). Thus, biblical studies have always been interested in the social context and the social rules that shape language.[8]

In recent years, biblical exegesis has been greatly shaped by a number of debates taking place in modern literary-critical circles.

The result has been greater attention given to the ways in which subjects (and objects) are schematized by texts and the ways in which texts are tailored to the interests and reading patterns of their audiences. Influenced by new ways of thinking about texts, biblical exegetes now acknowledge that not only is an audience's response an intrinsic component of meaning but that there are reasons why texts are structured in certain ways. For example, prophets chose one metaphor over another and then executed the metaphor according to principles known to them. Many of their decisions, we are discovering, were the result of assumptions the prophets made about their audiences and the conventions for writing/speaking within which both prophets and audiences operated. That prophets would have carefully tailored their language and imagery according to their audiences' preferences and competencies is obvious since, like all ancient speakers, prophets uttered their oracles not for art's sake but to arouse, to influence, to challenge, to inveigh against, and to politicize audiences. To succeed in their efforts, the prophets must have had definite notions of what their ideal audiences were like (e.g., their preference, tastes, temperaments, values) and the kinds of textual signals to which their audiences would respond.

In summary, to make themselves understood, the prophets Hosea, Jeremiah, and Ezekiel had, for the sake of argument, to describe marriage, gender roles, and women's sexual activities in ways that were intelligible to their audiences. They had to assume that their audiences would recognize as significant language and imagery that departed from expected modes of expression. In their choice and manipulation of marriage and sexual imagery, the prophets made definite assumptions about the cultural viewpoints of their Hebrew audiences—viewpoints that we moderns may or may not share.[9]

Female Powerlessness, Male Voyeurism

Sobered by these challenges, we now return to our question

about the audiences assumed in the speeches of Hosea, Jeremiah, and Ezekiel. What kinds of audiences did the prophets expect to be receptive to their messages and to hear them out? The first and most obvious feature of their imaginary audiences is that they were largely, if not exclusively, male. Only an audience that had never been raped or had never perceived rape or sexual abuse as a real threat could be expected to hear the kinds of ribald descriptions of abused women, sexual humiliation, assault, gang rape, violation, and torture that the prophets described and not recoil in fear. Only an audience that could relate to and identify with the metaphorical husband's outrage and horror could possibly perceive his reactions as plausible and legitimate. The prophets repeatedly employed the marriage metaphor to rationalize Israel's (impending) destruction and to show that Israel was getting what Israel deserved. Power, betrayal, punishment, violence, honor, and shame—these are some of the central themes in each prophet's use of the metaphor. Only those who had a certain relationship to power could appreciate some of the assumptions embedded in the metaphor. That is, the metaphor expected its audience to sympathize with the rights and responsibilities that came with power and to understand the threat that women could pose to male honor.

The image of the incorrigible, promiscuous wife played on male fantasies and fears of women's sexuality.[10] It is based on a way of thinking that sees women's bodies as mysterious and dangerous and perceives women's sexuality as deviant and threatening to the status and well-being of men. Indeed, the female body is always a point of contention within the metaphor: the woman insists on giving her body to other men; she has the temerity to dress herself in ways that call attention to her bodily self; and her punishment takes the form of rape, public exposure of her genitals, and the disfigurement of her body.[11] The metaphor takes for granted men's rights and power over women's sexuality; it reflects a fascination with female nakedness; and it assumes that the actions of men are somehow analogous to

God's actions.[12] In short, it is a metaphor most likely created by
the male imagination for the male imagination.

One might argue, in fact, that the metaphor of the promiscuous wife is the kind of metaphor Hebrew men shared with other
Hebrew men, in that it was a metaphor that absolved them of
guilt in battering their wives, a metaphor that perpetuated self-
serving lore about women and women's bodies, and a metaphor
that justified the control and punishment of women.[13] But the
point of the metaphor was not to tell them what they knew were
already defensible ways of treating and thinking about women.
Instead, the aim of the metaphor was to get the audience to see
the parallels between their fate and that of indecent women.
Much of the prophets' preaching was directed at the public
sphere of policy making—the policies and preachments of
kings, priests, scribes, merchants, and other prophets—but here
we find the prophets using a metaphor from the private sphere
of domestic and family relations to denounce what was going on
in the palace, the temple, and the marketplace. The metaphor
was clearly expected to have the power to pierce the sensibilities
of the men who dominated the public sphere by drawing parallels between their public decisions and the sexual (e.g., chastity,
childbirth, menstruation, rape) and moral world (e.g., fidelity,
subservience) of women. To paraphrase baldly this largely male
debate, the prophets' argument is this: God is as outraged at
what you're doing as any one of you would be if your wives were
acting the way you are acting. The metaphor was aimed at elite
Hebrew men, those who set the nation's moral and political
course; the prophets accused these men of acting like women—
and lusty, depraved, defiled women at that!

One can only imagine the shock and disgust that greeted these
prophetic messages. To compare the sublime social and religious decisions of elite men to the odious female bodily functions of women was itself surely insulting.[14] Using a metaphor
from the private sphere to denounce behavior in the public

sphere threatened to blur the distinction between private and public, with the result that the prophets supported the view that sex and power go hand in hand, and warned that, when left unchecked, both sex and power have the potential to undermine the identity of a nation.[15]

Virtually every culture has its own set of ideas about what is appropriate behavior for a man and what is appropriate behavior for a woman. In ancient Hebrew culture, in particular, part of what it meant to be a man was to protect the sexual purity of the women in the household—whether that be the sexual behavior of the man's wife/wives, his daughters, his sisters, even his mother. Women's sexuality was expected to be firmly in the hands of men. Male status and prestige rose and fell according to a man's ability to control the sexual activities of the women in his household. Honor, which evidently only men were capable of having, was accorded only to those men who were able to defend their family, who produced legitimate and numerous (male) heirs, and who exercised authority over the subordinates in their household (that is, wives, slaves, children). At stake, then, in the image of the outraged, avenging husband was not the husband's wounded pride, his fear of rejection, or his fear of a failed marriage—all of which are rather anachronistic ways of interpreting the metaphor. Actually at stake were the husband's honor and status as a man.[16]

Conversely, Hebrew women were expected to be modest, chaste, industrious, deferring, and willing to submit to male authority. Their virtue was best seen in the wisdom they exhibited in their roles as wives and mothers.[17] A woman who acted contrary to these expectations threatened the social order. More importantly, she brought shame and dishonor upon the man/men who ruled over her household (*bêt ʾāb,* "father's house"). In particular, a wife who engaged in sexual relations with other men threatened the purity of her husband's bloodline. The prophets portrayed Israel's relationship with God in marriage imagery in order to play upon men's fear of women's sexuality and their assumptions that women posed a threat to male honor and status. The prophets hoped that the male ruling elite might see parallels in the divine command for worship of the one God. Moreover, drawing analogies from customs of marriage and sex played down the monstrous ways in which the husband punished his wife and emphasized the fact that he was justified in restoring his honor.

The Feminization of Cities

Although each prophet used marriage and sexual imagery in his own way to comment on Israel's social, political, and economic policies, the prophets were not the first ones to feminize populations. The tradition of portraying cities as female was derived from the larger world of Ancient Near Eastern mythology. It was a common literary custom to portray cities, especially capital cities, as wives of the patron gods.[18] Like women, cities are not only weak and vulnerable to incursions, but also "the city contains the populace within her walls, nurtures it, provides for it, and defends it."[19] Because capital cities stood out from the rest of the terrain in their urban sprawl, their cultural, religious, and political importance, and their commercial traffic, female metaphors associated with them almost always cast them as grand, beautiful, fascinating, regal, and seductive places.[20]

The notion that the capital city was somehow uniquely attached to, protected by, and accountable to the patron god was a part of the thought world of the prophets and their audiences.[21] The prophets and their audiences were heir to this way of thinking about cities and women and borrowed from it in drawing parallels between God's reactions to Israel's idolatry and a husband's reactions to his wife's adultery.[22] Although the three prophets examined in this study directed their messages primarily to the capital cities of their birthplace (Hosea was concerned with Samaria, while Jeremiah and Ezekiel were concerned with Jerusalem), it is often difficult to determine when the adulterous wife refers to the capital city and when the image stands for the land or the nation at large.[23] One can only assume that the male audience to whom the speeches were addressed knew when to make the distinctions, or whether such differentiations were important.[24]

Whereas in Ancient Near Eastern literature the capital city was always spoken of in positive terms, in the literature of ancient Israel the capital city could be portrayed positively (e.g., Zion the Beloved)[25] or negatively (the loose, wanton woman) depending on whether the prophets wanted to vilify the city or arouse sympathy for the city. The image of Zion the Beloved found throughout Jeremiah, Lamentations, and Deutero-Isaiah was used to arouse pity and sympathy for Jerusalem, the tender girl who has been victimized, ruined, and left to mourn her loss. Zion became the helpless female in need of rescue (e.g., Isa 49:14–18; Jer 8:18–9:3; Lam 1:17; 2:1, 10). In contrast, the portrait of Jerusalem the adulterous wife shifted sympathy away from the city and in the direction of the husband/God as the one who has been victimized and betrayed. Here Israel became the degenerate, rebellious, and scandalous woman who deserved to be punished. This bifurcated image of Israel the female played into classic stereotypes in ancient and modern literature of woman as either "whore" or "virgin."[26]

Let us turn now to look at how the prophets shaped marital and sexual imagery from a literary point of view to tap into the attitudes and values of their audiences. How did marriage and sex relate to power and punishment? What kinds of attitudes and values did audiences have to pretend to share in order to accept the prophets' metaphorical use of marriage as a lens through which to view the relationship between God and Israel?

"Is She Not My Wife?"
Rhetoric and Audience in Hosea

Hosea is usually credited with being the first prophet to use the marriage metaphor to describe the history of the relationship between Israel and God. Hosea was building upon what was already an ancient way of talking about the deity's attachment and obligations to capital cities, but he expanded the imagery so that it could shed light on a whole range of thinking about divine–human activities. Whether Hosea had any impact on the people and events of eighth-century Samaria is difficult to say.[27] (Evidently, the prophet failed to persuade those in power to alter their behavior so as to avert the destruction that loomed before the tiny kingdom of Israel.)[28] What is striking, however, is that, of the prophets preaching at the time in Samaria—and certainly there were others besides Hosea—Hosea's prophecies are the only oracles by an eighth-century northern prophet to have survived.[29] Not only did they survive, but they went on to influence the preaching of later generations of prophets, notably Jeremiah and Ezekiel, in their use of marital and sexual imagery.

Hosea 2 opens by hurling the audience into the throes of a domestic dispute between a husband and his wife.[30] Their conflict is private, intimate, and painful to hear. In strong language the husband accuses his wife of adultery, and he enlists his children's help in bringing his wife to her senses.[31]

> Say to your brother Ammi,
>   and to your sister Ruhamah.
> Plead with you mother, plead—
>   for is she not my wife,
>   and am I not her husband?[32]

In this opening of the dispute, the audience was invited to listen and take sides. Following this accusation of adultery, the audience would be fascinated to see how this drama would play itself out. What course would this Hebrew man take? Will he divorce his wife?[33] Will he have her stoned to death as the law prescribes (Deut 22:22)? Another option, of course, not granted by the law but probably permitted in the culture, was simply to beat her.[34]

The Hebrew word *rîb*[35] ("dispute") gives legal connotations to the husband's accusation. Knowledgeable audiences would not have failed to pick up on the husband's insinuations. Nor would they have failed to notice the plaintive tone of his question posed to the children: "Is she not my wife, and am I not her husband?" (v. 4). One reason the husband was shocked by his wife's behavior is because it ran counter to well-established norms. In fact, the point of Hosea's rhetorical question is to symbolize for his audience how grossly illicit and abnormal was his wife's behavior. What she was doing, according to him, stood in direct contradiction to the customs and mores governing married women.

The legal and rhetorical tone of the question posed to the children allowed the husband to establish the frame and basis for his ensuing complaints against his wife. It also lent forensic force to his argument and gave it an air of authority and respectability. The prophet accomplished an important rhetorical feat here: he combined the best insights of two popular metaphors for divine–human relations: forensic and marital metaphors. Fundamental to both metaphors is the notion that there are duties and responsibilities that are intrinsic to human relationships. Those duties and responsibilities elevate human relationships from the realm of mere emotions and temperaments, claims and counterclaims, to an arena where one might engage in a systematic inquiry into justice, equity, and responsibility. The two metaphorical images tied together insist that with intimacy comes accountability. The wife has betrayed her covenant vows.

The allusions to the emblems draping the wife's face and breasts in 2:2 are oblique to the modern reader but probably were not to the ancient audience.[36] Just the mention of these emblems and explicit reference to the woman's body parts, especially her breasts, was surely enough to cause the audience to wince in discomfort. Nonetheless, coming as it does on the heels of v. 2, the threat in the following verse (2:3) to strip the woman as naked as the day she was born would not have been taken lightly by the prophet's audience. In a culture where nudity was an utterly private matter and where seeing anyone naked apart from one's spouse was a disgrace, the gravity of the prophet's words would not have been lost on his audience.[37] The implication of his threats is unmistakable: the wife's penalty (public nudity) will correspond to her sin (dressing in vulgar apparel). Not only that, but her impending nakedness (here the woman gives way to Israel) will be reminiscent of her former days in the wilderness (*bammidbār*), presumably before she knew her husband (God), before their marriage (covenant ceremony), when she was still lost and abandoned.

The husband was outraged both by his wife's illicit behavior and by the fact that she wrongly ascribed to her lovers what rightly was his alone to boast: the honor of being her provider and benefactor (vv. 7, 12). He accused her outright in v. 5 of acting like a whore (*zônâ*).[38] By becoming sexually involved with other men, she treated these others as though they were her husband. The husband did not bemoan the possibility that his wife no longer loved him; neither did he consider the possibility that the breach in their marriage may be his fault. Rather, he was outraged by her shameless, wanton behavior that brought dishonor on him in the eyes of other men. She humiliated him both by becoming involved sexually with other men and by claiming that they were the ones who provided for her.

No attempt is made to be specific about the nature of the wife's immorality other than to speak vaguely about her apparel, her sexual involvement, and the general esteem with which she held her lovers. The prophet's accusations against the men of Israel remain vague therefore. He was evidently confident, however, that the accusation, not the proof, of adultery was enough to get the attention of his audience.

Nevertheless, although the husband's accusations were vague, his threats were crisp and clear. He threatened to strip his wife naked and to kill her with thirst (vv. 3, 5), barricade her with thorns and a wall—presumably in her own home (v. 6), and then take back everything he had given her and leave her naked and empty (v. 9). There is no question of the husband's power in the relationship. He had the power as a Hebrew male to decide his wife's fate. He could divorce her, have her stoned to death, or, if he chose, beat her into submission. One wonders whether the prophets' repeated treatment of the metaphor was the result of their thinking that assault was the more humane punishment. Regardless, the husband's objective was clear: he would put an end to whatever illusion of security she had found in her new relationships (vv. 11–13).

Recapitulating his wife's words—or what according to him are his wife's words—makes the poem in Hosea appear almost dialogical, giving the audience the impression that he has attempted to reason with his wife, and, failing that, pleads with his wife to come to her senses.[39] Throughout the speech, the voice of God and that of the husband become virtually indistinguishable. It is impossible to tell where one ends and the other begins. The husband becomes confused with the deity, and a woman's sexual behavior is elevated to a matter of national policy. The festivals of mirth in v. 11 are the only concrete activity alluded to in the entire poem. Even there, the prophet remains vague about the wife's role in the festival.[40]

The shift from threats (vv. 1–13) to seduction (vv. 14–23) that follows only enhances the image of the husband as the true victim in the marriage. As the real victim, he is a man driven to extreme behavior by his unfaithful wife, and his monstrous violence against his wife in vv. 1–3 is almost understandable. At the same time, proof of his decency can be seen in the fact that despite what happened in the past he is willing to take his wife back.

In the second half of the poem (2:14–23), the prophet once again calls to his audience's mind the memory of the wilderness (2:14: *midbār*). This time, however, it is as a place of cherished memories from the past. Israel and God first cut covenant with

one another in the wilderness, a place of loyalty and mutual
devotion. Bygone days in the wilderness were sure to bring to
mind days of peace, accord, and stability. The prophet assumed
an audience that cherished the tradition of the wilderness. It was
a place of fond memories for Israel. It was a period in Israel's history, says Hosea, signified by faithfulness and oneness between
deity and people.

We have seen up to this point the prophet's skills as a poet and
demagogue. First, he captures his audience's imagination by
posing to them something of a dilemma: faced with an adulterous wife, what was the logical, conventional, sound thing for an
honorable man to do? The prophet suspects that the very notion
that the husband is willing to take his wife back, to reclaim her
after she has become defiled by other men, that he is willing to
start anew, and that he will trust her unconditionally again is
unimaginable to his male Hebrew audience.[41] Indeed, never
could his audience imagine that a husband might take his adulterous wife back so lovingly, so gently, with such trust. The only
place where the prophet seems prepared to give in to his audience's expectations, however, is when he shows the husband's
determination to retaliate physically against his wife before taking her back.

According to the poetry in 2:14ff., after a period of chastise-
ment their vows as husband and wife would be renewed and his
wife's devotion to him rekindled. In contrast to the first half of
the poem where marriage was used to convey the extent of
Israel's theological and moral estrangement from God, in the
second half of the poem the prophet used the marriage metaphor
to illustrate in tender, comforting, romantic language and
imagery what Israel's existence would be like reconciled to the
one God. Moreover, whereas her words in the first part of the
poem were central to the husband's complaints (vv. 5, 7, 12), in
the second part the wife's voice has yielded to her husband's
(2:16, 18). The rhetorical accomplishment of the second half of

the poem is its ability to replace the threats of violence with promises of romance. Whether he must threaten or seduce her, in the end, the husband/God will have the last word, not the wife/Israel.

By the end of the poem, the marriage metaphor has been extended to include the entire ecological order. Indeed, all of creation joins with the couple in a ceremony of renewal (vv. 16–23). The heart of this section is concerned with restoration and renewal. The promise of a restored, created order like the one envisioned in vv. 16–23, where the earth is in harmony with nature (peace) and with the heavens (rain), was an important one. The portrayal in vv. 16–23 of a restored, peaceful ecological and cosmic order (rain, peaceful coexistence with animals and with neighbors) resonated with the concerns of the tiny northern kingdom of Israel, which frequently found itself the victim of environmental imbalances as well as the target of foreign military intrusions (from Syria, Assyria, Babylon, and Egypt). By the end of the poem, the poet has come full circle. Marital strife has given way to harmony, and accusations have dissolved into reconciliation. Thus, the audience has been invited to ponder the imponderable. Those who once were condemned for their shameless disloyalty to God are promised that after an obligatory period of punishment there remains the possibility of restoration just beyond the horizon. Only a nation wrestling with loss and ruin, or the imminent threat of loss and ruin, could fully appreciate the pathos of the prophet's message.

We see, then, that the eighth-century prophet Hosea performed his rhetorical tasks skillfully. He captured in the marriage metaphor some of the most cherished cultural notions dear to his audience: power, honor, security, and justice. He manipulated stereotypical images of women in assorted sexual dramas to evoke a range of emotions in his audiences (e.g., shock, shame, fear, comfort, and horror). The success of Hosea's attempt to persuade his audience of their blatant disloyalty to the covenant that their ancestors had made with Yahweh (whether by aligning themselves with foreign powers or by absorbing foreign religious practices into the Yahweh cult) lay in his ability to use imagery of sex, romance, and violence to appeal to his audience's inherited cultural values, exploit their greatest fears, and evoke their most sacred traditions.[42]

"You Have the Forehead of a Whore"
Rhetoric and Audience in Jeremiah

Despite the one hundred years that separated the prophetic ministries of Hosea and Jeremiah, in many ways the audience presupposed in Jeremiah is similar to the one presupposed in Hosea. For both audiences, sexual infidelity and indecency in women were insufferable. Jeremiah's audience, like Hosea's, believed that extreme behavior in wives called for equally extreme behavior by husbands. Both prophets expected their audiences to share their contempt for immodest women, and both shaped the marriage metaphor around the assumption that husbands had the power to enforce their intentions upon their wives.

In Jeremiah's speeches, the metaphor of the promiscuous wife enhanced the highly emotional tone of the entire book. The tone of the book of Jeremiah is one of urgency, agitation, desperation, and frustration.[43] Indeed, in contrast to the first three chapters of Hosea, where the marriage metaphor predominates, marital and sexual imagery is scattered throughout the book of Jeremiah (2:1–3; 2:29–37; 3:1–5; 3:1–11; 4:29–31; 13:20–27; 31:31–34), with most occurring in the first four chapters of the book. In Jeremiah the attention appears to be less on developing a profile of a particular promiscuous woman (who, in turn, symbolizes Israel) than on evoking general visceral examples of loose female behavior (e.g., Jer 3:1–2; 4:30). The prophet uses the metaphor to underscore the point that sexual independence in women is lewd and disgraceful.

Jeremiah piled sexual image upon image and punctuated his message with rhetorical questions which may have been the poet's way of attempting to overwhelm the senses of his audiences. Either he believed that his audience was especially obdurate, or he felt that the historical crisis confronting his audience was pressing enough to call for extraordinary hyperbole.[44] The preponderance of rhetorical questions in the book of Jeremiah (for example, "What do you mean that you dress in crimson, that you deck yourself with ornaments of gold, that you enlarge your eyes with paint?" [4:30]) suggests that the prophet was so convinced of his position that he actually could not conceive of why his audience was unable to see the error of their counterposition ("Can a girl forget her ornaments, or a bride her attire?" [2:32]).[45] From a rhetorical point of view, then, the prophet Jeremiah used the marriage language not only to shock but also to quarrel and reason with what he felt was an especially dense group of men.

Despite the urgent tone of the prophet's message, however, the marital and sexual imagery in Jeremiah functions rhetorically in a different way than it does in Hosea. Beyond its ability to shock and capture the imagination and attention of its audience, beyond its ability to garner wide appeal based on universal assumptions about the place of wives and women, beyond its ability to tap into a wide range of emotions related to a tiny nation's need to feel protected and secure, the most conspicuous way in which metaphor is employed in Jeremiah is to provide a framework for evaluating Israel's behavior over a period of time. That is, the prophet uses the marriage metaphor to contrast the former Israel with the present Israel.

> I remember the devotion of your youth,
>   your love as a bride,
> how you followed me in the wilderness
>   in a land not sown.

Israel was holy to the L ORD ,
    the first fruits of the L ORD 's harvest.
All who ate of it were held guilty;
    evil came upon them.
(Jer 2:2b–3)

The prophet impresses upon his audience the notion that Israel's apostasy and rejection are appalling and painful because such behavior stands in stark contrast to the memory of the early days of their union in the wilderness, days marked by Israel's singular devotion to and love for God. The prophet's oracles deliberately open with this imagery of Israel's former devotion so as to set in his audience's mind the criterion by which Israel's present behavior would be gauged: "I remember your (previous) devotion" (2:2b; cf. 31:32).[46] It explains the husband's dismay: "Can a girl forget her ornaments, or a bride her attire? Yet my people have forgotten me days without number" (2:32). He attempts to get his audience to understand that in light of Israel's past devotion, its current, flagrant disloyalty becomes all the more shocking: "What do you mean that you dress in crimson . . . ?" (4:30). Her shocking licentious behavior provides the rationale for her punishment: "If a man divorces his wife and she goes from him and becomes another man's wife, will he return to her? Would not such a land be greatly polluted?" (3:1). In fact, punishment becomes unavoidable because the wife has proven herself incorrigible: "How long will it be before you are made clean?" (13:27).

In Jeremiah, the norms governing male honor and female modesty were unassailable. As surely as a remarried woman could not return to her first husband (because she has become defiled by the second husband), so Israel could not possibly think of returning to God (3:1). Just as red apparel, gaudy jewelry, and heavy makeup were inappropriate for modest women, so Israel's superficial attempts to improve her looks and stave off her destruction and ruin (4:30) were ludicrous and obscene. As surely as having her skirts ripped above her head was humiliating to a woman, equally appalling was the judgment of God that awaited Israel for its abominable ways (13:25–27). Only an audience who shared the prophet's firm beliefs about female propriety and sexuality could be persuaded by his analogies.

Although numerous poetic images are used in Jeremiah to capture God and Israel's relationship (e.g., son, house, meadow, choice vine, field, daughter), images used principally to characterize the nature and extent of Israel's apostasy, none had the symbolic potential to startle and shock an audience, one imagines, as much as sexual imagery. The prophet even enlisted animal sexual imagery to reinforce his portrait of Israel as audacious and incorrigible, comparing the latter to an insatiable animal in heat (see 2:23–25; 5:7–9).[47] Both female imagery and animal imagery were used to convey dismay at and disgust for Israel's actions. But whereas the wife in Hosea came across as naïve and deceived (2:5: "I will go after my lovers; they give me my bread and my water, my wool . . ."; 2:8: "she did not know that it was I who gave her . . ."), the woman in Jeremiah lacks innocence; she is stubborn and well aware of her decisions ("How well you direct your course to seek lovers!" [2:33]). In fact, the specific aspect of the woman's behavior that the image of the promiscuous woman makes clear but which imagery of animals in heat cannot convey is that the woman *is* culpable, accountable, and responsible for her behavior (3:3b). An animal is not. The implication is that Israel/the wife deserved to be punished but that it would be senseless and futile to punish an animal. The speaker sounds thoroughly exasperated with the woman when he asks bluntly and crudely: "Where have you not fornicated?" (3:2a).[48] (This question must surely have stopped the prophet's well-bred audience dead in their tracks!)

In Hosea, the wife was an adulterer; but in Jeremiah she was a prostitute, a whore, a slut. Since he seemed interested in using the metaphor to talk about decency more than marriage norms, less attention was given by Jeremiah to drawing out the figure of both wife and husband. The voice of God and the voice of the prophet were one in their critique of Israel/the woman. The prophet constructed his rhetoric not only to draw a direct parallel between the woman's sin (shameless, loose behavior) and her punishment (exposed and shamed) but to insist that her punishment was reasonable and inescapable. How could Israel expect to escape punishment? the prophet wondered aloud (2:29; 5:7–9), when she has been so intractable in her sins. If the prophet believed his audience was especially obstinate and dull-hearted, he seemed hopeful that sexual imagery would help him penetrate his audience's senses.

To make them understand fully the impact of the ruin that awaited them, the prophet forced his male audience to endure the scene of a woman having her clothes snatched above her head (13:20–27). For men who placed great value on the chastity of virgins and the sexual fidelity of wives (cf. Deut 22:13–30), to hear the threat of a woman having her private parts exposed to the public must have been both curious and unsettling. It was strong imagery, meant to signify the shame, humiliation, and indignity that awaited the prophet's audience (13:26ff.). The inference in chap. 13 is that while it will be her (political) lovers, Assyria and Egypt, who will ravage and expose her secret abominations (vv. 20–21), God the husband remains the powerful one in that God allows Israel's lovers/allies to destroy her (vv. 26, 27). However, the shame that the prophet attempted to etch in the audience's imagination was the shame of having been publicly exposed (13:26) and the shame of having been betrayed by one in whom one has trusted (2:37).

The prophet Jeremiah used female bodily scenes to accent the emotional side of the divine–human drama. Israel's betrayal of the Sinai covenant was not just a legal matter, something that called for a calm, rational, straightforward response from God.

Betrayal was also cause for profound emotions to erupt: disappointment and shock. Rhetorically constructing the woman as a prostitute allowed the prophet to convey how shocking, scandalous, depraved, and downright unnatural were Israel's actions. Men who were charged with the task of proclaiming justice, interpreting law, and dispensing wisdom (e.g., 2:8, 26; 5:4–5; 8:8–12) had begun to act in ways that defied everything that was natural and rational (e.g., 2:11, 14; 5:7–9; 5:30). They were acting like whores! Their ways, according to the prophet, threatened the very fabric of Israel's existence. It was enough to make the prophet weep (8:22–9:3).

In Jeremiah as in Hosea, the image of the loose woman served ultimately as a device to announce judgment and salvation. By reminding Israel, in the opening chapters of the book, of the strength and glory of her former days when she loved and adored God alone (chap. 2), Jeremiah made the day of their future reuniting all the more attractive and persuasive (chaps. 30–31). Once their marriage vows had been renewed, Israel's new relationship with God would exceed the former: "but I will make a new covenant . . . not like the old covenant . . ." (Jer 31:31–34; cf. Hos 2:16–23). In the undisclosed future, her former sins forgiven and forgotten, Israel would know her husband/God more intimately than ever. Presumably, the knowledge Israel would have was knowledge that would ensure her future security, status, and longevity.

In short, the marriage metaphor became a rhetorical device for Jeremiah to connect Israel's past, present, and future. According to André Nehrer, "the structure of conjugal symbolism is that it localizes the past, situates the present, projects the brief future, gives to the succession of time the signification of history."[49] Thus, for the prophet Jeremiah, the marriage metaphor, as a device for announcing judgment, was a suasive instrument for gauging how far Israel had strayed from her earlier covenantal commitment and pledge. At the same time, as an instrument for announcing salvation, the metaphor became a suasive instrument for symbolizing for Israel the gains and benefits of repentance.

Jeremiah's rhetorical imagery presupposed an audience that failed to see the connection between its past and its present, an audience stunned by its (imminent) ruin. The prophet brought all of his prophetic rhetorical powers to bear to remind his audience that while it was true that their punishment (13:20–27) corresponded to their sin (2:30–37), the hopeful message nonetheless was that it was possible for Israel to be reconciled to God with a reunion not simply reminiscent of its past bond in the wilderness, but based on a better covenant (31:33–34). Thus, Jeremiah evokes in chap. 2 the memory of Israel's former devotion (1) to contrast how depraved Israel had become; (2) to contrast the past failures of the covenant with the future triumph of the covenant; and (3) to point to something concrete in her past that would remind the nation of the benefits of remaining devoted and loyal to God. The prophet envisioned an audience that shared his rigid beliefs about female modesty and wives' fidelity to their husbands. Any behavior in women and in Israel that deviated from these principles was threatening to the social order, deviant in nature, and warranted severe punishment. At the same time that the prophet construed his audience's behavior as abominable and shameless, he also used romantic imagery to reassure them of something equally astounding: namely, *after a period of punishment*, God stood prepared to forgive Israel and to begin their relationship anew.

"The Lady Is a Tramp"
Rhetoric and Audience in Ezekiel

The prose speeches in Ezekiel 16 and 23, where the marriage metaphor is concentrated, bring us face to face with the artistry or literary character of prophetic discourse. At last we have an opportunity to consider how marriage, sex, and violence are brought together into a full-fledged epic drama about courtship, estrangement, betrayal, punishment, and reconciliation. The prophet Ezekiel uses the life cycle of one experience (marriage) to contemplate the cycle of another experience (the historical relationship of Israel and Yahweh). Whereas in Hosea and Jeremiah images, sometimes two or three verses in length, follow in rapid succession upon one another, in Ezekiel entire chapters are given to the careful, more extended development of a metaphor as a way of describing yet another aspect of Israel and God's relationship.[50] With chapters of quite substantial length one is able to see the considerable potential of the metaphor to convey numerous aspects and nuances of God and Israel's stormy relationship. Most notably, the prophet is able to develop with more explicitness what remains in the realm of allusion in Hosea and Jeremiah: first, how the people came to be God's special choice; second, the nature of their idyllic life together as devoted bride and generous, protective husband; third, the details and extent of the wife's subsequent downfall; and, fourth, the possibility of her restoration. In short, in Ezekiel, extensive elaboration upon the husband and wife's relationship allows the metaphor of the promiscuous wife to provide a biographical framework for tracing a people's history with their god from courtship to marriage to adultery to punishment to reconciliation.

The *dramatis persona* in Ezekiel is Jerusalem. The capital city is the promiscuous wife. The prophet details the city's rape, violation, and humiliation. Like Jeremiah, Ezekiel overwhelms his audience with one image after another, offending every sense of decency and propriety his audience must have held, exploiting each element of the metaphor for its ability to represent adultery, harlotry, and humiliation. The prophet goes to great lengths to detail the extent and nature of Jerusalem's punishment. Whereas rape was mostly only alluded to by the other two prophets, it and other sexual activities become decidedly explicit in Ezekiel.[51] In fact, so extensive is the prophet's commentary on the woman/ Jerusalem's ruin that many of the prophet's descriptions fall into the category of what some today might classify as pornographic. He refers openly to a woman's pubic hair and developed breasts (16:7), as well as to her menstrual cycle (16:10). He describes gang rape in great detail (16:37), talks about coital emissions (23:8), and even throws in a reference to the size of the lover's sexual organ (23:20). (This kind of language is enough to make even modern audiences blush.) Many times his lurid descriptions are so candid and protracted they threaten to blur the boundaries between preaching and raving.

Ezekiel assumed a great deal of knowledge on the part of his audience. Although he and his audience were among those who had been forced to go to Babylon as prisoners of war (3:12–15), the prophet expected his audience to be very knowledgeable about political and religious matters back in Jerusalem. He expected them to be aware of and know about Jerusalem's dealings with Egypt, Assyria, Edom, and others (16:23–29; 23:22–35). Perhaps he was drawing on his audience's background as persons from royal, patrician, and merchant-class backgrounds who once ruled and administered Jerusalem's political and religious institutions (Ezek 1:1–3; 2 Kgs 24:10–17). Second, and more subtly, the prophet assumed that his audience was able to discern when he was referring to political abominations, when cultic abominations, and when general moral decline—or whether such distinctions were necessary. Third, like his predecessors Hosea and Jeremiah, he assumed that his audience looked down on promiscuity in women and expected women engaged in this kind of behavior to be properly punished.

Here we find that the husband's voice and perspective dominate the entire drama. The use of the first-person verb in both Ezekiel 16 and 23 allowed the husband to insist that what would happen to the woman was at the husband's behest.[52] The husband was not overpowered; the husband in fact surrendered his wife to the consequences of her lust for unsavory relationships (16:58; 23:49). Ezekiel used marriage and sexuality to emphasize the notion that the husband had absolute authority and control over his wife. Marriage and sex, then, became the canvas on which the metaphor was used to reinforce in his audience's mind notions of power and powerlessness, authority and submission, and honor and dishonor. A male audience was expected to empathize with Ezekiel's description of some of the most obscene, most misogynistic impulses conceivable against women.

At the center of Ezekiel's message in both chapters is the insistence that the wife's flagrant dealings with foreign lovers/allies brought dishonor upon her husband. For her crimes against her husband, she herself would be put to shame and mocked by the same lovers/allies she once sought to impress. The body she used to seduce and ensnare her lovers would become the same body her husband would use to bring her down. It is the principle of *lex talionis*, an eye for an eye. The husband exchanges his dishonor for his wife's disgrace. In fact, in both chaps. 16 and 23, the prophet repeatedly refers to the odious nature of Jerusalem's ways, and in both he also uses body imagery to rationalize Jerusalem's demise. The female body is used to conjure up for Ezekiel's audience images of dread, chaos, anarchy, and evil.

Although the prophet used the marriage metaphor to compare and contrast Israel's behavior, his interest was not simply in Israel's history. His interest in sin provided his audience a lens through which to view Israel's *reputation* over a period of time (compare Ezek 16:14 with 16:57 and 23:32–34). Indeed, she who had once been clothed by God in splendor and dignity (16:14) had become debased in ignominy and shame (16:57). The details of her renown (16:1-14) were matched by the details of her debauchery (16:15–34; 23). It was the story of one woman's slow descent into immorality and depravity: her journey from being orphaned, to being found, cleaned up, and having fame bestowed upon her by her generous benefactor and husband (16:1–14), to becoming loose and promiscuous, engaging in increasingly abject and smutty practices (16:15–34; 23:5–21), and finally to being raped, battered, and mutilated (16:6–52; 23:22–49).[53] The prophet in chap. 16 left no doubt in any one's mind that the wife's punishment was her own fault.

Again and again, he emphasized the woman's own whorish[54] ways as the cause of her ruin. Her husband gave her over to the impulses of her depraved lovers. Her reputation was tarnished, and she became "an object of reproach" and a byword to all those around. According to chaps. 16 and 23, Jerusalem has become a mockery and a song of taunt (16:51; 23:32–34). Taken together, the two narratives themselves function as a taunt against the woman, a type of speech intended to mock, deride, and jeer at her for her lewd behavior. Indeed, the careful and laborious rehearsal of her demise is itself supposed to be mocking and insulting.

Part of the prophet's objective, evidently, was to see to it that his audience understood the full implication of their deeds—presumably, so as not to repeat them.[55] To do that, Ezekiel brought all his prophetic and rhetorical skills to bear on the task of influencing his audience's thinking. By reminding them of their former glory, describing in lurid details Jerusalem's abominations, comparing their sins to that of their lesser sisters (Sodom and Samaria), describing in ghastly images Jerusalem's degradation, he inflamed his audience and even insulted them. The language and imagery seem to suggest an audience that took great pride in Jerusalem's reputation and splendor. They also assume an audience invested in protecting and managing Jerusalem's reputation—an audience that had overseen Jerusalem's national and international policies—perhaps the personnel of the royal court (rulers, scribes, civil servants, priests, and aristocrats), those who were knowledgeable about Jerusalem's intrigues with Egypt, Assyria, and others. They were the very ones who had grown arrogant in assuming that Jerusalem's special place in God's heart was unconditional.[56]

Only one of the two narratives (chap. 16) uses the marriage metaphor to foretell Jerusalem's future restoration. And even there, the allusion to Jerusalem's restoration is as acrid as the description of her fate (16:59–63). The prophet did not go into great detail about the woman's restoration. In fact, the section comes across as a parenthetical aside inserted for good measure. Perhaps little attention was devoted to the matter in order not to encourage any hopes that return was imminent. The prophet seemed more interested in proposing that, should Jerusalem's fortunes be restored, it would be because *God had remembered God's everlasting covenant with the people and had forgiven them their sins* (16:60). It was not the result of anything Jerusalem had done. In the meantime, the memory of her downfall, her public humiliation, her reproach among her neighbors should serve as a permanent warning in Jerusalem's mind (16:61).

Finally, the language and imagery of Ezekiel 16 are reminiscent of Hos 2:4–13, and the language and imagery of Ezekiel 23 brings to mind portions of Jeremiah. The former emphasized profound betrayal, and the latter hopeless depravity. In both chapters of Ezekiel, however, in contrast to Hosea and Jeremiah, the drama of romance and rape does not involve simply a husband and a wife, but involves a husband (Yahweh) and his two co-wives (the sisters Samaria and Jerusalem). The husband contrasts the behavior of his co-wives and recapitulates his judgment against each wife. When outlining the depravity of Jerusalem, he recounts how since the days of her youth Jerusalem too had permitted men to fondle and caress her breasts, how in turn she had catered to her well-endowed, lust-filled paramours; and how as her husband he subsequently lost his desire for his wife and handed her over to her lovers. The inference is that certainly any self-respecting, honorable Hebrew male could understand what a man in the husband's circum-

stances felt like. Thus, the image of the promiscuous wife in
Ezekiel reinforces the notion that the wife had somehow dishonored her husband, misconstrued his generosity for weakness, and underestimated his power over her as his wife. In the
end, she would learn painfully, cruelly, horribly that so unrelent-
ing is her husband's claim upon her, and so absolute is his power
over her, Ezekiel insists, that God her husband can be as cruel in
his punishment as he was compassionate in his beneficence.

Conclusion

This inquiry into marital and sexual imagery has examined
how the prophets used language of romance and violence to
exert emotional power and influence over their audiences' thinking about their culpability and God's justice. Explicit sexual language and disgusting scenes of a sexually ravaged woman were
intended to convince the prophets' audiences that they had no
one to blame but themselves. Each played on cultural stereotypes
about women to evoke strong reactions of shock, horror, and disgrace in their audience. The prophets were not content to make
cerebral arguments against sin, anarchy, and breach of covenant.
They were adamant and used imagery that reflected their intense
feelings. To their thinking, God's claim upon Israel was itself so
absolute, so non-negotiable, so relentless that any infraction was
intolerable and damnable. The strict norms governing women's
lives were one way for the prophets to make their point.

In particular, the prophets shaped their messages to enforce
several important points. First, they drew both political and
semantic correlations between Israel's sins and Israel's fate. By
describing her punishment (rape, exposure, battery, shame) in
language and imagery that echoed the language and imagery
used to describe her sin (promiscuity, immodest apparel, stub-
bornness, and shamelessness), the prophets made indelibly
clear that God was not to be blamed. The wife was responsible

for her actions. Scandalous actions, so the rhetoric goes, deserve scandalous reactions.

Second, the cycle of female sexuality provides an excellent analogy with which to capture the shifting fortunes of Israel's history with God, a history of relations that were often erratic and unstable. From the vulnerability that comes with being a newborn to the sexual awakening that emerges during puberty, from the passion that characterizes bridal love, to the utter shame that accompanies rape, and from the forlornness that follows abandonment to the assurance that comes with reconciliation, Israel the child, girl, wife, harlot is represented rhetorically as a woman whose emotions over the generations have been erratic and undependable. Thus, as ancient rhetorists the prophets were careful, on the one hand, to exploit every detail of the woman's gradual slide into debauchery and dissolute behavior. On the other hand, they could depict God as profoundly patient, imploring, and shocked by his wife's behavior (e.g., Samaria and Jerusalem). Personifying Israel as a woman permitted them to call into question their audience's false assumptions about their innocence and integrity and their flawed assumptions about God's justice or God's power.[57] In a patriarchal society that closely regulated female sexuality, by feminizing Israel as an adulterous wife the prophets insisted foremost that the wife (people) was (1) a social reprobate, (2) responsible for her actions, and (3) deserving of her punishment. We see then that the marriage metaphor became an important rhetorical tool for defending God's reputation and for addressing Israel's repeated questions about theodicy, suffering, and the inscrutable ways of God.

Third, and related, in this chapter we have seen repeatedly that the prophets were intent on tapping into a broad range of emotions and passions to make their points. Both human and divine emotions were metaphorized. A range of contradictory feelings was tapped into: love and anger, contrition and shame, humiliation and disappointment. From the two narratives in Ezekiel, as well as portions of Hosea and Jeremiah, we witness the tenderness of God's compassion, the shamelessness of the woman's abominations, the depth of God's disappointment, the terrifying nature of God's anger, and, finally, the inscrutableness of God's love. And if emotions are not logical, then love is even less so, say these ancient rhetorists. They insisted with imagery of marriage, sex, and violence, therefore, that God as well as Israel could be unpredictable in response; in fact, after God's avenging wrath, God could turn unexpectedly, compassionately toward Israel/ Jerusalem to restore her and to renew God's vows with her.

The prophets were not trying to use rational, logical, coherent, reasonable, detached arguments to get through to their audiences. (Speeches laced with sexuality do not lend themselves to neat, rational arguments.) The language and imagery the prophets Hosea, Jeremiah, and Ezekiel used were often erratic, evocative, and unpredictable, leaving the arguments with the semblance of moving from *absurdum* to *absurdum*. The change in the prophets' thinking was as emotionally motivated as it was intellectually motivated (Jer 31:31–34). Theirs was a war of language, using all their rhetorical skill to polemicize against everything from moral and political idolatry to national upheaval and colossal ruin. They expected their audiences to hear them out. They spoke with all the passion, hyperbole, and drama characteristic of speakers who doubt whether they will be given another chance to speak. They expected what they had to say to do something to their audiences.

We can only imagine the reactions of elite Hebrew men upon hearing their actions compared to female infidelity (Hosea), to sexual lewdness in women (Jeremiah), and to women's impurity (Ezekiel). To be compared to a mangled, mutilated, ravished, raped, nude female body must surely have left such an elite group filled with mixed reactions. As shrewd rhetorists, the prophets counted on their audiences' mixed reactions to shape their message and to drive home their points. Their mixed reactions would only underscore the ambivalent character of their dilemma. With reactions ranging from intrigue to repulsion, horror to outrage, from desire to shame, the audience was sure to grasp the depth of their disloyalty and the depth of God's own disappointment and heartbreak over the deeds of God's covenant people. The strong, complicated emotions they were sure to feel would, it was hoped, persuade them to see the rationale for their punishment and convince them never again to conduct themselves as if they were impure, depraved women.

3

"Am I Not Her Husband?" The Unpredictable and Unimaginable God

Our focus in the previous chapters has been on exploring the ways in which the prophets Hosea, Jeremiah, and Ezekiel used the trope of female sexual promiscuity to denounce and ridicule the public behavior of their male audiences. We have centered our attention on the ways in which the prophets manipulated a hodgepodge of assumptions from the domestic sphere—namely, the role of wives and male dread of and desire for female sexuality—to debate the morality of activities taking place in the public sphere of politics and religion. We have seen how the prophets craftily appealed to the image of the depraved wife and the dishonored husband to characterize what they saw as the idolatrous practices of elite Hebrew men who in their offices in the cult, the court, and the palace shaped the moral vision and set the political course of their tiny nation. Expecting their male audiences to subscribe fully to the notion that women's sexuality posed a threat to male prestige in that it potentially undermined power, property, and purity distinctions, the prophets accused their audiences of conducting themselves in the manner of a wife turned whore. The prophets depended on their audiences' reactions of shock, horror, and disgust at hearing themselves compared to degenerate women to impress on them the extent and gravity of their disloyalty to their covenant god. In particular, the prophets' used the metaphor of the promiscuous wife to rationalize divine retribution and to symbolize the shameful and scandalous demise of a once-great nation.

Despite the role women play as metaphorical subjects in prophetic literature, there is rarely any mention by the prophets of the actual lives of women.[1] The sphere of home and family was rarely a central topic in prophetic discourse. In fact, aside from an oblique comment here and there, one finds hardly any denunciations of wrongdoings in the private realm where women's lives were largely confined. As far as the prophets were concerned, the most urgent matters were the breaches taking place in the public realm of temple, palace, court, and, in some cases, the marketplace. These were the spheres of prophetic scrutiny—the world of kings, scribes, priests, and wise men— the spheres where God presumably acted out God's purposes for human history. For only in androcentric activities might one perceive the intentions and purposes of God for a society. When the prophets did refer to women in their speeches, their interest was in women's deeds and fate as the mothers, sisters, daughters, or wives of men.[2]

If the prophets' aim in metaphorizing sexual promiscuity was simply to caricature elite male officials and to characterize their actions as absurd and disgraceful, it would have been enough perhaps simply to draw analogies between male malfeasance and the actions of an incorrigible whore. But the point of the metaphor was not merely to characterize Israel's behavior— however inane its actions and however fatal its course. What was problematic for both prophet and audience alike—and what drove prophets time and again to rely on metaphors—were the actions of God. The point of prophetic metaphors was to shed light ultimately on divine activity. And while they were never at a loss to explain what motivated Israel to act in certain ways, the prophets (and audiences) were frequently hard pressed to explain why God did what God did or failed to do what Israel expected. Imagining Israel as the promiscuous wife and God as the dishonored, outraged husband became a way for prophet and audience to contemplate and explain Israel's experience with a God whom the people perceived at times to be actively engaged in their history and at other times to be deafly silent to their pleas.

It is not surprising that sexuality became a central metaphor for Israel's self-conception, with marriage, adultery, and fidelity acting as prominent themes both for Israel's national identity and for Israel's relationship to God. The prophets perceived "a thread of similarity" between the anxiety that sex typically arouses in an audience and the profound disease, instability, uncertainty, and ambiguities that lay at the heart of Israel's struggle for a national identity.[3] The story of Israel's past, which included Israel's attempts to interpret and construct that past, is the story of what one scholar has termed "the dilemmas of desire, the struggle between contradictory attractions, rather than the history of a monolithic dogma. As such it is the story of a profoundly ambivalent culture."[4]

Sexuality proved, however, to be an apt canvas on which many of the dilemmas that perpetually faced the tiny, struggling nation could be inscribed and represented. Israel was preoccupied with defining its borders and constructing for itself a national fiction, and its authors repeatedly framed sexuality within geopolitical and international contexts. From the original divine blessing to "be fruitful, multiply, and fill the earth," to the tale of two daughters who deceived their father Lot into engaging in illicit sexual relations with them and who in turn gave birth to eponymous sons Ammon and Moab; to the story of Ruth, the great grandmother of King David, whose tale embodied a problematic congery of themes—death, sex, procreation, fertility, erotica, and the foreign woman; to the repeated injunctions in both law and narrative material against intermarriage and the going astray that ensues when the holy seed is mixed with the peoples of the land; to the story of David's rise to power and his involvement in a wretched affair with another man's wife; to the feverish speeches made by the prophets using the marriage metaphor to remonstrate against male activities—human sexuality repeatedly threatened to undo the fragile myth of kinship and solidarity that defined the nation, forcing the mythmakers to find language and symbols to constrain the nation's contradictory impulses. One might argue, then, that anxiety about sexuality and the threat it posed to households and borders functions as a countercohering theme for a great deal of the Old Testament.[5]

But sex proved not only to be an ideal trope for contemplating Israel's identity as a nation. It also proved to be an apt metaphor for representing Israel's volatile relationship with God. Unlike the other four frequently used metaphors in prophetic speeches, the marriage metaphor, because of its elaboration on the complex nature of human intimacy, was able to capture some of the more disturbing aspects of the relationship between Israel and God, one being the nation's long history of fickle and unreliable devotion to Yahweh their God. Greater still, however, was the metaphor's ability, rooted as it was in the capriciousness of marital love, to rationalize Yahweh's volatile, erratic dealings with Israel. No other metaphor had the potential to capture this confounding side of the deity's relationship with Israel, a side that left prophets, priests, and scribes frequently scrambling for an answer. Without the analogy of marital love, the interpreters of Israel's theological traditions were hard pressed to explain what sometimes must have felt like the unpredictably abusing side of God.

For example, the husband of the marriage metaphor comes across as a deeply ambivalent man, one who can be as cruel and pitiless toward his wife as he can be gentle and giving. He is at once seductive and menacing. He is at times deeply moved by the nation's despair and fiercely devoted to the nation's deliverance. At other times, he comes across as heartless in his retribution and deaf to the cries of the people. Situating the nation's history with God within a drama of infidelity and spousal abuse allowed the prophets Hosea, Jeremiah, and Ezekiel to draw parallels between God's stormy dealings with Israel and a husband's stormy dealings with an adulterous wife. That is, while God's love for Israel was profound, God's potential to become angry and jealous was not to be taken lightly. After all, the God who creates weal in Israel is the same God who is capable of creating woe in Israel (Isa 45:7); and the God who sends prophets "to build and to plant" is the same God who sends prophets "to pluck and pull down" (Jer 1:10). Like a jealous husband who has been humiliated by his wife's affairs, God was capable of taking some unimaginably harsh measures against Israel his wife. God is described as an abusive husband who batters his wife, strips her naked, and leaves her to be raped by her lovers, only to take her back in the end, insisting that when all is said and done Israel the wife shall remain interminably the wife of an abusing husband, "and I will take you for my wife forever" (Hos 2:19). The portrait of the husband (God) in the marriage metaphor therefore is far more complicated than some interpreters have been willing to admit. He is not simply hurt, desperate, or jealous of his wife's infidelities. He is outraged, menacing, and unpredictable in the measures he takes against her. Here the prophets admitted that Israel's history had shown repeatedly that God was as capable of being abusive as God was of being compassionate.

The suggestion that the marriage metaphor calls attention to Israel's experience of God as unpredictable might seem to be at odds with the use of the metaphor to give coherence and rationality to God's history with Israel. The marriage metaphor brought figurative coherence to the various cycles in Israel and God's relationship (courtship, marriage, betrayal, punishment, and reconciliation) and permitted the prophets to draw a connection between Israel's crimes (whoredom and adultery) and Israel's punishment (rape and nakedness).

As prosaic as God and Israel's history may have seemed in the imagery of the marriage metaphor, drawing as it does similarities between Israel and God's relationship and the well-known cycle of intimacy-estrangement-intimacy that humans endure in marriage, the picture of God as an outraged, humiliated, and menacing husband was always just beneath the surface of the poetry, threatening to make God appear irrational. At times the metaphor seemed almost to get away from the prophets (especially in Ezekiel, where the husband leaves his wife to be abandoned, raped, mutilated, and humiliated). Where the woman's rape, battery, humiliation, and assault are elaborated upon verse after verse, God is not simply punishing Israel; God seems to be out of control.

> Therefore, O whore, hear the word of the Lord: Thus says the Lord God, Because your lust was poured out and your nakedness uncovered in your whoring with your lovers, and because of all your abominable idols, and because of the blood of your children that you gave to them, therefore I will gather all your lovers, with whom you took pleasure, all those you loved and those you hated; I will gather them against you from all around, and will uncover your nakedness to them, so that they may see all your nakedness. I will judge you as women who commit adultery and shed blood are judged, and bring blood upon you in wrath and jealousy. I will deliver you into their hands, and they shall throw down your platform and break down your lofty places; they shall strip you of your clothes and take your beautiful objects and leave you naked and bare. They shall bring up a mob against you, and they shall stone you and cut you to pieces with their swords. (Ezek 16:35–40)

> Therefore, O Oholibah, thus says the Lord God: I will rouse against you your lovers from whom you turned in disgust, and I will bring them against you from every side: the Babylonians, all the Chaldeans, Pekod and Shoa and Koa, and all the Assyrians with them, . . . they shall come against you from the north with chariots and wagons and a host of peoples; they shall set them-

selves against you on every side with buckler, shield, and helmet, and I will commit judgment to them, and they shall judge you according to their ordinances. I will direct my indignation against you, in order that they may deal with you in fury. They shall cut off your nose and your ears, and your survivors shall fall by the sword. They shall seize your sons and your daughters, and your survivors shall be devoured by fire. They shall also strip you of your clothes and take away your fine jewels. So I will put an end to your lewdness and your whoring brought from the land of Egypt; you shall not long for them, or remember Egypt any more. For thus says the LORD GOD: I will deliver you into the hands of those whom you hate, into the hands of those from whom you turned in disgust; and they shall deal with you in hatred, and take away all the fruit of your labor, and leave you naked and bare, and the nakedness of your whorings shall be exposed. Your lewdness and your whorings have brought this upon you, because you played the whore with the nations, and polluted yourself with their idols. (Ezek 23:22–30)

Although all three prophets went to great lengths to insist that Israel's punishment corresponded to Israel's actions, they did not deny the fact that sometimes the punishment was exceedingly cruel. But that was the price of living in covenant intimacy with God. In fact, in Ezekiel the husband does not apologize for his rage, knows of no restraints in the punishment he metes out, and even fully intends to brutalize his wife until he feels satisfied and avenged:

> . . . I will stop you from playing the whore, and you shall also make no more payments. So I will satisfy my fury on you, and my jealousy shall turn away from you; I will be calm, and will be angry no longer. (Ezek 16:41b–42)

His accusations against his wife are protracted, and what he proposes as her punishment is carefully premeditated. So painful and brutal is the punishment he imagines for his wife (e.g., rape, dismemberment, and humiliation) that in the end the husband comes across looking as crazed as his wife is wanton. The implication is clear: there is no reasoning with a husband who has been humiliated and rejected by his wife. By portraying God as menacing, stalking, and cruel, the metaphor of Israel as promiscuous wife and God as outraged, dishonored husband highlights Israel's experience of God as the source of both good and evil. The prophets were careful to acknowledge that just as God was capable of profound acts of mercy and compassion, there was also a side to God that was mysterious and adversarial.[6] It was not the result of any flaw in God's character; it was part of the unsettling mystery of being in relationship with God and part of the risk taken when in relationship with one who was, according to all of Israel's metaphorical thinking about God, a dominating Other. Whether God was king, master, judge, or parent (or shepherd or warrior, for that matter), God, in all the prophets' representations, was ultimately powerful, sovereign, and always somewhat Other-than those with whom "he" entered into relationship.

We see, then, how the marriage metaphor was able to absorb two rather contradictory sides of Israel's experience with God: the side of Israel's history that showed God as devoted husband, compassionate and advocating on the nation's behalf, and the side that showed God as jealous husband, abusive and unpredictable. Curiously, the prophets did not feel compelled to resolve these contradictory portraits of God. They were aware of the fundamental tension that existed in these contrasting portraits of God and were willing to live with these tensions as intrinsic to what it meant to be in relationship with a power overwhelmingly greater than oneself, a power that alone determined the parameters and fate of the relationship. God was fundamentally unpredictable, the prophets insisted, and was therefore not obligated to be confined to the imaginations of the human heart.

No matter how many similarities the prophets scrambled to come up with to show that God's relationship with Israel was not incoherent or incomprehensible, each prophet insisted ultimately that God reserved the right to act according to precepts God alone understood.[7] After all, says God, according to the prophet Hosea, "I am God and not man" (11:9).[8]

Moreover, portraying God as simultaneously devoted husband and jealous husband underscored the point that God was not a mere spectator to Israel's existence nor to her fate. God was, according to all the prophets, intimately attached to Israel and deeply affected by Israel's actions: God pleads with, rails against, threatens, assaults, and reembraces Israel—just like a husband. Although God was prepared to act on Israel's behalf to save Israel, God was equally prepared to act against the nation to destroy it: "she did not know that it was I who gave her the grain, the wine, and the oil . . . . Therefore I will take back my grain in its time . . ." (Hos 2:9). Indeed, marriage and female sexual imagery allowed the prophets to paint a portrait of a god who felt intensely and reacted passionately, a god who was profoundly devoted to Israel but at the same time deeply offended by Israel's acts of impropriety. Marriage, then, becomes something of a two-edged contract: there are the explicit, mutually agreed upon stipulations laid out in the covenant, and there is the jumble of implicit conditions, unspoken expectations, and irrational needs that lie just beneath the surface of human intimacy.[9] It is precisely these unarticulated and inarticulable codes and emotions that make all relationships—but especially ones bound by intimacy—volatile and erratic.[10] The metaphor of Israel as wife may have allowed the prophets to capture Israel's depraved, fickle behavior; but the metaphor of God as husband also permitted the prophets to capture the inexplicably menacing, dark side of God's dealings with Israel.

After descriptions of punishment, however, the portrait of the outraged husband gives way to the image of the romantic wooing courtesan. Each time the husband's menacing accusations and threats are followed by lush gestures of courtship and romance, making the husband's opening threats seem less dangerous and brutish—and more the overreactions of a distraught and heartbroken man. Likewise, in the face of his wife's wanton, obscene betrayal, despite his almost perverse delight in detailing his savage retaliations against his wife, the husband in Ezekiel 16 and 23, for example, comes across as much as a victim of his love for his wife as his wife is a victim of his battery. The implication is that no matter how extreme or erratic may be God's reactions to Israel's idolatry, God in the end is as much a victim as Israel is. In other words, when Israel is punished God suffers as much as Israel suffers.

Only the marriage metaphor allowed audiences to glimpse the image of the impulsive, volatile, ambivalent Hebrew man. Male characters in the Old Testament may act impulsively from time to time or may be allowed emotional outbursts on occasion—but only in the metaphorical portrait of the Hebrew husband does the reader find consistent images of the out-of-control Hebrew man. In a culture that prided itself on a canon of precepts given by the deity to ensure some measure of order and decency in all realms of the lives of its citizens, it is curious that here in the domestic realm of marriage and intimacy one finds persistent images of the raving, unrestrained Hebrew man. One gets the impression that it was precisely here in the domestic realm of male and female relationships, in the realm where control over the sexuality of the women in one's household was important to male honor, considerable latitude was permitted husbands to avenge whatever damage adulterous wives might do to their honor and prestige.[11]

Finally, the metaphor of the promiscuous wife and avenging husband represents more than the prophets' attempt to address questions posed throughout Israel's history about divine goodness and theodicy. Indeed, the matters taken up by the marriage

metaphor went far beyond the question of God's power and simple goodness. It was the question of God's unpredictability that
preoccupied this metaphor. The picture painted by the marriage
metaphor of God, of life, and of divine–human history was complex and discomfiting. The prophets agreed that the punishment
meted out to Israel sometimes exceeded the crime, that Israel
was often left to the vilest impulses of their enemies, and that
God sometimes remained deaf to Israel's protests and expostu-
lations. The marriage metaphor admitted that God's ways were
often inscrutable. But, according to the prophets, God's abuse
and unpredictability were not to be construed as defects in God's
character; rather, they are part of the messiness of intimacy.

God, Gendering, and Power

Our interest in the marriage metaphor concerns not only
what it purports to convey about the character of God's relation
with God's people but also the way in which the metaphor
belongs within a larger cultural context of imagining the power
that sustains and structures a society. One of the reasons the
marriage metaphor made sense to ancient audiences was
because many of its fundamental ideals coincided with the views
audiences already held about the world, about God, about gender roles, and about power. It concurred that God was male. It
upheld belief in male power and female subjugation (already
assumed and taken for granted throughout scripture). It capitu-
lated to the idea of a violent, retaliatory God already promul-
gated in other prophetic metaphors (e.g., king, judge, master). It
maintained male prestige and honor codes. Moreover, it sanc-
tioned a world that both elite and common men would have a
vested interest in preserving, a world of power and privilege over
women. With the marriage metaphor, power remained firmly in
the hands of the powerful; a hierarchical worldview was maintained; and the right of the powerful to retaliate physically
against those less powerful remained unquestioned.

In addition, by casting wives as prurient, faithless, and obdurate and husbands as generous, pleading, and forgiving, the prophets reinforced existing stereotypes about gender relations in marriage. Directing their messages to male audiences, they catered to a prevailing desire of those in power to see themselves as the real victims in marriages and thus to justify their turning to violence. Indeed, as fascinating and as provoking as the marriage metaphor may seem to modern interpreters, and as shocking as its detailed descriptions of sex must have seemed to ancient audiences and must seem to modern audiences, the marriage metaphor was in many respects a relatively conservative poetic device for imparting religious teachings. It supported the status quo in a patriarchal world and left unchallenged male power over and aggression against women.

Audiences ultimately cling to some metaphors (and not others) because they reflect the known world. They also cling to some metaphors (and not others) because of the metaphors' ability to persuade them to think about their old contexts in new ways. Indeed, a good metaphor is one that is able to push an audience to think about a subject in new ways. Before the marriage metaphor was introduced into Hebrew thinking, Israel perhaps had not thought of its relationship with God in such personal, intimate terms; nor perhaps had Israel comprehended the contractual nature of that relationship and the shame and honor that were attached to its stipulations. While the metaphor of the promiscuous wife did not challenge men's relations to women, it did force men to see themselves and their relations with God in ways they had never seen before. Talk about adultery, breasts and genitals, semen emissions, menstruation, the male phallus, and scenes of childbirth, rape, sexual flirtation, and humiliation was an effective poetic ploy precisely because it forced the audience to think about themselves in both repulsive and fascinating ways. It did this by "bring[ing] unlikes together, upset[ting] conventions, involv[ing] tensions, . . . [making it] implicitly revolutionary."[12] In an otherwise modest culture, where social intercourse between the sexes was rigidly legislated, such candid portrayals of sexuality surely shocked and provoked the imaginations of the prophets' audiences. To characterize elite, socially prominent Hebrew men as whores and to imply that there was very little difference between them and sexually impure women must have caused quite a stir, to say the least.

For a prophet to combine lurid sex talk with talk about the God of Israel, a masculine-gendered deity—but one scrupulously unassociated with any sexual characteristics—must have been outrageous. To associate honorable Hebrew men with sexually vulgar women and to ask those same men to imagine themselves in an erotic relationship with God was unthinkable.[13] This was the kind of talk that landed prophets in stockades. But when history proved Hosea, the first prophet to use this imagery, correct—Samaria was destroyed; the land was laid waste; and it was all the result of Israel's interactions with foreign protection—prophets afterwards could not help contemplating Israel's history in similarly subtle and nuanced ways. If nothing else, they had to see Israel's relationship to God differently. That is, while it may have been insulting to be compared to women, marital and sex talk did drive home the point that the nation was getting what it deserved and that to love God and to be faithful to God called for those responsible for charting the course of the tiny province to see themselves in ways they had never imagined before: powerless, weak, defiled, undependable, possessed—in a word, female.

Monotheism

It is difficult for us to appreciate how important the marriage metaphor was to the prophets' overall rhetorical purposes. They convinced Israel that reliance on any god apart from the God of Israel was futile, wrong, ludicrous, and dangerous. No other metaphor could capture, reinforce, and symbolize the notion that Israel belonged only to Yahweh the one God, the God Israel's ancestors had pledged long ago to worship. The nation had become by the time of the prophets incorrigible, lax, and slack about its duties to its God. To stress the special, unique, and exclusive relationship required by Israel's God, the analogy of marriage was ideal. Whereas a man could be husband to many wives, a woman could be the wife of only one husband. Likewise, just as a Hebrew male expected absolute sexual loyalty and devotion from his wife/wives, so God expected Israel's exclusive devotion.[14] Worship of other gods was absolutely intolerable.[15]

Furthermore, while the marriage metaphor admitted to God's mysterious, unpredictable side, it also allowed the prophets to talk about a kind of radical monotheism that in the end shifted the blame for disaster and evil away from God and placed it squarely on the shoulders of human beings. Prophets centuries after Hosea, even beyond the prophecies of Jeremiah and Ezekiel, continued to revive marital and sexual imagery and saw in it a fascinating trope for prophetic proclamation about human obligation to the deity. The marriage metaphor, with its intense preoccupation with exclusive devotion and loyalty to one husband, would prove to be a helpful lens through which they and their audiences could view what they might see as the causes of the nation's demise.[16] According to the metaphor, Israel's destruction was the result of the nation's tendency to worship and rely on foreign gods.

Finally, whatever positive insight is to be gained from the metaphor's portrayal of divine punishment is in its theology of evil. The metaphor insists that good and evil are intimately related. In fact, God is capable of both good and evil, just as life itself is capable of heaping good and evil upon one's head. Evil and disaster, so says the marriage metaphor, are the flip sides of intimacy and joy. Moreover, evil and disaster are not "out there," somewhere outside of human beings, outside of history, waiting to overtake human beings. Evil and disaster are close, intimately near, within one's most intimate spaces, in one's own heart perhaps. The god unveiled in the image of the menacing husband is one Israel was willing to face and own as its own, although it is one moderns hardly know how to talk about. We don't know how to talk about that presence in our world—both inside us and outside us—that is neither friend, lover, father, mother, redeemer, companion, or cocreator.[17] How do we talk about the terror that is divine? With its insatiable appetite for danger and destruction, it stalks us in floods, earthquakes, fire, disease, and irrational violence. Powerless kingdoms are quick to submit to a god who delivers and obliterates. They maintain that both ill fortune and good fortune are from the same source. The God of the Old Testament, argued the prophets, is one who for no apparent reason turns on one, a God aware of one's helplessness and vulnerability before encroaching powers, a God who does not save, does not protect, and does not obliterate one's enemies. Hence, however one might take exception to the image of God as abusive and destructive, one must commend Israel for its courage to grapple with the dark side of human history, the dark side of God, and the dark side of intimacy.

Finally, in all of this Israel never lost sight of the role the nation played in its own demise. There is plenty of evidence throughout the Old Testament that despite its understanding of the universe as imbued with divine presence, Israel was well aware that the greatest threat to its existence was not divine but human.[18] Israel was destroyed not simply because God was unpredictable, but chiefly because Israel had transgressed God's covenant. In other words, God was unpredictable, but Israel was stubborn. God sometimes chooses not to rescue God's people, but instead leaves them to the vilest, most inhumane, most destructive impulses of other human beings. But even when God so chooses, it does not mean that God has given up on God's people. God remains powerful, compassionate, and uniquely devoted to Israel, says the metaphor. At those times, God suffers and anguishes with Israel in its calamity (after all, the husband is as distraught and out of control as the wife is broken and humiliated). More surprising is that, after a period of punishment, God stands ready and willing to comfort a weeping nation (Rachel), dry her eyes and reward her for her trials with an invitation for renewal (Jer 31:16–34). To modern audiences the God of the marriage metaphor may be much too violent to endure. But to Israel it was a portrait that was too honest and consistent with reality as they knew it to deny.

4

"Yet I Will Remember My Covenant with You" The World of Romance and Rape

In this final chapter we turn from examining the ways in which the prophets used the marriage metaphor to shape the thinking of their intended audiences—namely, Hebrew men—to considering the metaphor's implications for and effects on *unintended* audiences. The world of the prophets Hosea, Jeremiah, and Ezekiel was one where men had absolute power over women's bodies, a world where women's sexuality was considered threatening and dangerous to male honor, a world where rape and mutilation were potentially erotic, and where battery and rape culminated in romance and reconciliation. As clever rhetorists, however, the prophets must surely have suspected that there would be members of their audience who would question whether the parallels they drew between public policies and women's sexuality were fair, reasonable, or accurate. What they probably did not suspect—because they never had any reason to do so—was that their audiences might question the very morality of the metaphor. That is, the prophets probably never imagined themselves talking to audiences that would object to the metaphor's depiction of women, its assumptions about female sexuality, and its justifications for assaulting women. This brings us to a question undeniably at the heart of this and similar studies on biblical imagery, and that is what to do with a metaphor that promotes a world that is hierarchical, that demonizes and marginalizes women, and that rationalizes violence, a world that many modern readers cannot—even for the sake of argument—abide.

If the image of a promiscuous and raped wife fails to be fully convincing to a lot of modern readers two millennia and more after it was first introduced, it is because some readers are no longer willing to submit uncritically to the ethics, assumptions, and visions enshrined in the imagery. Indeed, part of the privilege of reading is that one has the opportunity to step back and weigh an argument, accepting portions of the argument and rejecting others. But to resist the almost irresistible rhetoric of prophets such as Hosea, Jeremiah, and Ezekiel calls for more than merely excavating the social and historical origins of the language they use (which has been the focus of the previous chapters). To resist rhetoric of rape and romance one must break the hold that images of battered, mutilated, naked female bodies have over the imagination. To break their hold means taking seriously the influence that romance, the erotic, and religious texts exert upon our culture. Part of that requires examining how the metaphor colludes with larger structures within our own culture (both material and theoretical) and how it taps into prevailing values, attitudes, and prejudices.

Put simply, what does pairing divine judgment with rape and battery of women do to audiences who are unwilling to live in such a world? What effect does reading descriptions of women battered, mutilated, and raped as a poetic device for divine judgment have on audiences who have been raped and battered and who live daily with the imminent threat of being raped and battered? These questions turn our attention away from rhetorical tactics of authors to the reading tactics of audiences.[1]

Texts affect different audiences differently. Some of the variations in reaction can be attributed to gender. For example, it is quite possible that descriptions of women's rape and battery do not affect women and men in the same way.[2] This means that the imaginative worlds the prophets proposed to female audiences would have been different from the ones they proposed to male audiences. Female audiences were asked in the prophets' speeches to endorse a world where their rape and mutilation were normal, legitimate, and conventional ways for men to assert their power over women. It was a world where husbands had power over their wives to do with them whatever they wanted, where husbands forgave their wives' adultery, wives forgave their husbands' battery, and both lived happily ever after. Whether women in ancient Israel could have identified with the lurid descriptions of women's rape and mutilation that appear again and again in prophetic rhetoric is a question that has been carefully avoided until this point, but now must be faced squarely. And the answer on one level is obvious.

There is no reason to doubt that the world of brutality, rape, and subjugation that the marriage metaphor assumes was a world with which Hebrew women were well acquainted. Indeed, the overwhelming evidence of Hebrew laws and narratives is that women were subordinate to men in both the public and private domains.[3] Not only is male dominance assumed in the Old Testament; it is not questioned. As one writer has pointed out, "[male dominance] was part of the social order of the world that the Bible did not question. The Bible has a new religious vision, but it is not a radical *social* document."[4] This means, then, that not only does the metaphor of the adulterous wife play upon male fantasies and fears about female sexuality. The metaphor also reinforces androcentric notions about wives as husbands' property and promotes patriarchal visions of marriage as a hierarchical arrangement where husbands clearly have the upper hand. The image of the battered promiscuous wife caters to patriarchal thinking in that it leaves unquestioned husbands' presumption that they have the authority to degrade and silence their wives when the latter act in ways that allegedly bring shame on their husbands. Therefore, there is no reason to believe that the rhetorical world the prophets proposed to ancient Hebrew women through the marriage metaphor was purely a creation of the prophets' literary imagination. There is no reason to suspect that the marriage metaphor had no basis in Hebrew social reality.[5] In all likelihood, the world of romance and rape taken for granted in the prophets' sexual rhetoric was not a world inconceivable to ancient Hebrew women. Indeed, in a world where it was conceivable that women could be made to marry their rapists, it is quite possible that women also found themselves having to reconcile with husbands who battered and mutilated their bodies.[6] Thus, it is quite imaginable that women in biblical antiquity—to the extent that they were permitted to stand in the squares where prophets harangued or were allowed into religious quarters where prophets shouted their proclamations—did not find the speeches preposterous, unimaginable, or beyond the pale of possibility. Speeches that romanticized and rationalized the random rape and mutilation of women in the name of divine judgment were probably not unthinkable to Hebrew women.

But to say that the image of the promiscuous and raped wife was comprehensible to female audiences in ancient Israel is not to say that it did not meet with any resistance within those ranks.[7] There may have been women in biblical antiquity who in their own ways took great exception to the rhetorical portrayals of battered women, but their resistance probably went unnoticed or was dismissed by men. But rhetoric, no matter how persuasive, is still just that—rhetoric. It still has to pass the tests of audiences. That is, audiences ultimately decide on the merits of authors' literary strategies and prophets' religious ploys.

There is evidence in biblical literature that there were women who understood the power of rhetoric. They understood the danger and potential of rhetoric to sway audiences' thinking and even to distort reality. We find several examples of women in the

Old Testament who opposed patriarchal rhetoric by denouncing androcentric edicts and by challenging what they believed to be illegitimate claims to power.[8] There is no reason to doubt that these women were representative of a small number who would have objected to the prophets' eroticization and rationalization of violence against women. These women knew that rhetorical rape can be as dangerous as actual rape and that language does indeed shape reality.[9] Rhetorical, or literary, rape is especially menacing because it teaches audiences how to imagine women in humiliating situations and how to perpetrate violence against women.[10]

Unfortunately, we do not have access to the writings of biblical women to test out our assumptions. We are forced to speculate that (some) ancient women heard the metaphor of the promiscuous wife differently from the way (some) men heard it. We are left to hope that they found ways to resist this rhetoric—if only to walk hurriedly away from the ranting of obscene prophets. We have only our own modern experiences to draw on, fully aware that there are worlds of differences between our lives (my own life, for one, as a North American woman of African ancestry who was born in the southern part of the United States and now teaches at a southern university) and the lives of ancient Hebrew women. Female readers in modern times, nevertheless, continue to be shocked, outraged, and frightened by the violence against women that goes virtually without comment in the Bible. Indeed, one of the reasons feminist scholars return again and again to this metaphor is in an attempt to demystify the language and undermine its hold on our imagination.[11]

Till Death Do Us Part

One cannot deny that generations of readers have been fascinated by and attached to the marriage metaphor. The reasons for this are many. Some have to do with the way readers have all been socialized: we have been taught to identify with the intense anti-woman sentiments found in much of classical literature, including the Bible. To read many of the classic texts of Western literature, one must be willing to identify with male interests and male values and not question the absence of strong women, not notice that those women who are strong wind up killed, branded, or left insane. We must not think it odd that in classic literature whereas women find their identity in marriage, men in search of themselves find their identity by first deserting the women they are related to (e.g., mothers, wives, sisters). In other words, the image of the subdued wife and the conquering husband is a familiar scene in Western literature.

But social conditioning to a male perspective accounts for only a part of the reason why readers see in marriage the epitome of the divine–human bond. We have also been taught to identify with the metaphor's utopian vision of romance and reconciliation. The portrait of the reconciled husband and wife caters to what we have all been taught to believe in—the strength of the family and the power of love. In its own misguided and disturbing way the marriage metaphor expresses that love triumphs in the end over catastrophe and destruction. The metaphor reassures us that love conquers all and that marriage is forever. No matter how bad things get in a marriage, there is always a possibility that love can be rekindled, vows renewed, and the marriage restored. Here, the betrayed forgives the betrayer, the battered forgives the batterer, and everyone lives happily ever after. Symbolizing more than just power and punishment, the marriage metaphor has come to embody some of our most cherished hopes as a society. As a literary trope, it has endured because it also appeals to what is perhaps a universal desire—to read literature that is inspiring, literature that leaves us feeling more optimistic about the future and about our own lives than we did before we read. Despite the vast differences in our life-styles and in our views of the world, and despite whatever ambivalences modern audiences might have about texts that romanticize violence, both ancient and modern readers can identify with the metaphor's portrayal of the vicissitudes of love, the pain that intimacy causes, the wounds that family relations inflict, and the healing power of forgiveness. One can hardly resist its portrait of love that triumphs over adversity.

The image of the promiscuous wife and the hand-wringing husband touches readers at some of the deepest levels of our conditioning. It assures us that relationships that have suffered a profound breach in trust can heal and triumph over their adversity. Not only does such an imagery reassure readers in the domestic sphere of their lives; it also comforts readers as citizens of a commonwealth. It promises readers that it is possible for a nation to find security and to regain its greatness amid towering superpowers. For Israel, the metaphor dramatized the notion that no matter how far the nation strayed from God there remained the assurance that God would remember God's covenant, forgive the nation, and restore order, stability, and peace to its borders. The idea of God's unconditional love prevailing over human failure and weakness has made the image of God as husband and humankind as wife a sacred way of imagining the divine–human bond. The marriage metaphor insists that domestic abuse can be redeemed through romance, seduction, and courtship. Never matter that the woman's punishment is brutal and borders on the pornographic. Never matter that the punishment in many respect exceeds the crime. The point is that the metaphor lures audiences into believing that despite their hopeless abject ways, there is a God who ultimately loves them and cares for them so much that—after a brief period of punishment—God will forgive them and reunite with them.

The Vulnerable Male

So hauntingly commonplace is its portrait of the ups and downs of marital intimacy that one almost forgets to question

the morality of the battery the woman endures. The reconciliation of husband and wife is described in such tender, heart-
warming ways that it is almost easy to forget that retaliation,
according to the metaphor, is a prerequisite to reconciliation.
The fact that the entire marital drama is told from the perspective of a man is not insignificant. Everything we know about this
marriage is told by the husband; it is a love story from a man's
point of view. The story of love, seduction, betrayal, abuse, and
reconciliation narrated by a brokenhearted man can seem fascinating to readers accustomed to the portrait of the stoic, detached,
sensible man. In their construal of marriage as a metaphor for the
divine–human bond, the prophets provide readers with one of our
rare glimpses of the man in love, the sick man, hand-wringing,
pleading, and heartbroken. It is an image in classic literature usually reserved for women. His nostalgic longing for the early days
of their marriage and his account of his desperate attempts to
reason with his wife offer us a portrait of male vulnerability. If
modern audiences have tended to overlook the husband's threat
against his wife and his rationalization of how to deal with his
depraved, stubborn wife, it is because we, like our ancient ancestors, have tended to find stories about men in love irresistible. In
fact, it is usually only in affairs of the heart that men are permitted to be irrational, out of control, and vulnerable. The world
of women, sex, and heterosexual love repeatedly threatens in
classical literature to undo great men (for example, the stories of
Samson and Delilah, David and Bathsheba, Mark Antony and
Cleopatra), leaving them to suffer the loss of their reputation
and their position, and to be perpetually distracted from their
true purpose in life. The image of the strong, stoic male is so
deeply embedded in our patriarchal cultural heritage that the
legal system in this country and elsewhere in the world has failed
to punish in any consistent manner men who batter wives and
lovers. The image of the jealous, controlling, possessive husband
is one of the most popular images there is of the man in love. We

can forgive him almost anything, even violence against those whom he loves. This point can be illustrated by looking at how each prophet neutralized the extravagant violence against the promiscuous wife with what may seem to some equally fantastic depictions of male longing, love, and romance.

"I Will Seduce You"
Romance Rhetoric in Hosea

Nowhere is the image of the battered but romanced wife more cleverly deployed than in the book of Hosea. Only in Hosea does the emotion evinced in the oracles of destruction (2:1–13) match the emotions evinced in the oracles of deliverance and salvation (2:14–23). The strident, menacing mood of the first half of chap. 2 gives way to gentle, seductive wooing in the second half of the chapter. Indeed, in vv. 1–13 the husband hurls one accusation after another against his wife, denouncing her as an adulterer and threatening to humiliate and kill her before those she claims are her lovers. But by vv. 14–23 he is no longer imagining his wife's death; instead he is looking forward to their reconciliation, when she will acknowledge him as her husband and true benefactor. The juxtaposition of the two speeches, one filled with disdain and threats of punishment and the other filled with affection and promises of reconciliation, balances the emotions. The gentle, seductive tone in the second half of the chapter all but compensates for the vicious threatening tone earlier. By the time his promises come to a close in vv. 14–23, the husband in the eyes of a reader is no longer a threatening, menacing stalker. He is a man who temporarily lost his composure and overreacted. He never meant to murder his wife, despite his threats; instead, his words in vv. 1–13 were the innocent desperate pleading of a man in love. Understood in this way, then, when the husband imagines in 2:14 luring his wife into the wilderness and talking sweetly to her, the husband's earlier threat to strip her and leave her as barren as a wilderness is no longer as threatening as before.[12] It was simply the harmless rambling of a man who was tormented by his wife's betrayal. What audience does not sympathize with the torment of love?

Further, many of the same extended metaphors from the natural world in 2:9–13 are alluded to and assumed in 2:18–22. In the former, the husband hisses at the nature festivals the wife takes part in, and threatens to banish her from them and from any other rituals that might occupy her time. To deflect attention away from his previous threats of isolating her, the husband turns around in 2:13f. and describes their reunion in language reminiscent of an outdoor wedding ceremony. Wild animals, birds, creeping animals are all invited to join with them in this covenant-making ceremony, witnessing their oaths and sharing their joy.

In the end, despite their differences, love triumphs over battery—or so the logic of the unit goes—and mutuality prevails over mutilation. The measures the husband takes, as violent as they might be, only demonstrate the extent to which a man of honor is prepared to go to preserve his marriage. The rationale for the husband's otherwise extreme behavior is clear: "This is what I did for love."[13] Audiences who value marriage over divorce are sure to empathize with the husband's distress and shame, and those who are moved by images of a man desperately in love will forgive and understand him (and God) for his bouts of irate jealousy. After all, the very fact that the husband in the book of Hosea elects to "reason" with his wife and does not opt to divorce his wife or to have her stoned to death is further proof of his benevolence. As for the assault, well, who doesn't know that love sometimes drives a man to do foolish things?

"I Have Loved You With An Everlasting Love" Romance Rhetoric in Jeremiah

In the book of Jeremiah, images of female sexuality, marriage, and promiscuity are scattered throughout the brief poetic units in the book. In many cases, units are hardly developed enough to show a systematic development of an idea. We have already seen how the brief allusion to the marriage metaphor in Jer 2:2–3 functions as a preamble to idealize a specific moment in Israel's past (the Exodus-Sinai wilderness) and to provide a standard against which subsequent behavior is measured. In other words, 2:2–3 sets the tone for the rest of the book in that the prophet allows the romanticization of Israel's past to conjure up a range of emotions, attitudes, and values that had to do with marriage, family, and romance against which all subsequent images, scenes, and counterarguments in the book would be weighed.

In Jeremiah, promises of reconciliation do not follow immediately on the heels of threats of exposure and humiliation as they do in Hosea. The book of Jeremiah is largely devoted to threats, warnings, and laments over Jerusalem's impending and actual ruin. In the first twenty-five chapters of the book, which are filled largely with poetic oracles, one finds only scattered hints of the possibility of Israel's renewal (e.g., 3:11–18; 16:14–18; 18:1–16; 23:1–8). Indeed, there seems to be a deliberate attempt to prevent any false hopes that Jerusalem had any chance of remaining intact (e.g., 8:8–13; 14:13–16; 18:18; 23:9–40). Not until Jeremiah 30–31 is a sustained attempt made to describe in grand terms the possibility of God's forgiveness and Israel's restoration.[14] The nation's hope and renewal are at the outset summed up by God's pledge of God's undying love, "I have loved you with an everlasting love; therefore I have continued my faithfulness to you. Again I will build you, and you shall be built" (31:3–4a). In these chapters and verses, female imagery abounds as the prophet describes the rapture, the joy, the comfort, the marvel, and the permanence of Israel's restoration. The image of the promiscuous wife gives way to that of Beloved Zion. The images that parade before the audience are of women poised for healing: the incurably wounded Beloved Zion abandoned by her lovers, left vulnerable and unattended, who is now promised restored health (30:12–17); the exultant virgin, who upon hearing of her benefactor's unceasing love takes her tambourine in her hands and dances (31:2–6); mother Rachel, consoled and reassured about her children's welfare (31:15–17); the women encircling warriors (31:22).[15] The emotions stereotypically associated with women (e.g., hysteria, glee, giddiness, excitement) are characteristic of the emotions exuded in the time of restoration.

In Jer 31:31–34 the prophet actually describes the nature and character of Israel (the wife) and God's (the husband) renewed covenant. It will be a renewed relationship based on mutual knowledge and trust. Female imagery is noticeably absent, even though scholars have long noted that the Hebrew word *yd*ᶜ, "to know" (31:34) connotes the knowledge acquired through intimate contact. Marital imagery is implied throughout the unit, surrounded as it is by language of romance and reconciliation. On one occasion, in v. 32, the speaker even identifies himself as Israel's "husband" (*ba*ᶜ*al*, "lord"). According to this passage, Israel and God will renew their relationship with a stronger, better covenant built on profoundly intimate knowledge of each other, replacing the former marriage which has been all but annulled by the wife's former transgressions. All of her sins have been obliterated from her husband's memory.

What audience can resist such love scenes? Who would be callous enough to hold the husband's former anger and bitterness against him? Who could possibly doubt his honor? After all, he who loves much forgives much. The distraught husband in the first chapters of Jeremiah has been replaced with the generous-hearted husband, and scenes of female debauchery and promiscuity have been replaced with heart-rending scenes of emotion-filled mothers and virgins. The prophet was confident that the sight of women content to find meaning in their lives as mothers, wives, and virgins would be comforting and irresistible—enough to make one almost forget their past indiscretions.

"My Fair Lady"
Romance Rhetoric in Ezekiel

Ezekiel 16 and 23 are two of the most violent chapters in the whole of the Hebrew Bible. In a testament full of stories of wars and punishment, nowhere is a person or group's ruin so lavishly detailed and described as it is here in these two chapters of Ezekiel. Here the imagery of sexual violence permits the author to exploit the potential sex has to generate a range of emotions in his audience: fear and worry, shame and guilt, and contempt and prejudice. The implication is that punishment and destruction extract as great an emotional toll upon a people as they do a physical toll. Going beyond Jeremiah, however, Ezekiel is interested in the marriage metaphor's ability to portray Israel as deviant and incorrigible.

The woman's punishment in Ezekiel is so savage and outrageous that it is difficult to imagine anyone hearing of her plight and not feeling empathy for her and disgust at the way she is treated. It is almost impossible to believe that anyone could conclude that this woman, or anyone else for that matter, deserved to be treated as cruelly as she is in the Ezekiel narrative (e.g., stripping her, gang raping her, hacking her, cutting off her nose, slaughtering her children). What kind of audience did the author imagine would find this brutality to be a just recompense for adultery? Who could have harbored such hostile misogynistic feelings against women, even promiscuous women? What kind of audience would not pause to protest that the punishment in no way fits the crime?[16] Who is convinced by the summary "'You must bear the penalty of your lewdness and our abominations,' says the LORD" (16:58), or "They shall repay you for your lewdness and you shall bear the penalty for you sinful idolatry; and you shall know that I am the LORD GOD" (23:49)? Finally, who benefits from such cruel treatment of women?

A relatively brief amount of attention is devoted to Israel's reconciliation and renewal in Ezekiel 16 (16:59–63), and there is no reconciliation drama in chap. 23. The prophet appears to have concentrated most of his attention on justifying the wife's demise rather than imagining the reunion of the couple. There is more interest in arousing sympathy for the dishonored husband than in pointing to the possibility of a reconciliation. The prophet goes to great lengths in chap. 16 to describe the husband's honor and his endless expressions of generosity and compassion toward his wife. It began when he rescued the woman as a foundling child, cleaned her up and cared for her, and lavished gifts upon her (vv. 1-13). She matured into a beautiful young woman and became his fair lady, of sorts. Whatever status and reputation she acquired were the result of his largess and compassion, not the result of anything the woman had done on her own (v. 14). Despite her husband's generosity, however, the fair lady abused her husband's love and brought dishonor upon him by pursuing affairs with other lovers. She indulged her every imaginable depraved desire, including sacrificing her children to foreign gods.

It is clear who the victim really is in this sordid drama: the husband. No matter how cruel the punishment of the woman may seem, it is the husband's wounded honor that is uppermost. The husband was clearly provoked and driven to retaliate by his sense of pride and honor. Enraged by his wife's failure to appreciate his generosity and aggrieved that she plays the whore with every passerby (v. 15), the husband is supposedly justified in whatever measures he takes to restore his reputation. He gave his wife over to her lovers, who raped and ravaged her.[17] Ezekiel the narrator was probably aware that the punishment exceeded the crime; the prophet elaborated on every detail of the woman's demise so as to emphasize the point that the woman got more than she deserved. He hoped to evoke sufficient horror and disgust at the woman's treatment to buttress his argument: God can be as insanely violent and jealous as God can be merciful and loving.

In Ezekiel the story of the adulterous wife is not told with an interest in portraying the triumph of love over disaster. It is a story of the triumph of power over defiance. The power the husband (re)asserts over his wife is more an illustration of his might than a testimony to any renewal of intimacy. It is a story of a woman who is brought to her senses and who acquiesces to her husband's authority. Rather than describing a reconciliation based on romance and seduction, like those in Hosea and Jeremiah, the prophet focuses here on the woman's profound sense of humiliation and shame as the basis of their getting back together. The prophet heaps detail upon detail of spousal abuse in the hope of dissuading his audience from acting in ways parallel to an adulterous wife. It is not, according to modern standards, a romantic story. But it is an idealistic story in that it imagines power restored, control regained, and a wife's obedience renewed. According to the prophet, it is understandable that a husband who has been disgraced by his wife temporarily loses his composure and allows his wife to be subject to her lovers' depraved advances. After all, a man can take only so much.

Resisting Romance and Rape Rhetoric

We have seen the ways in which the marriage metaphor diverts attention from its violence and directs readers' attention to its vision of reconciliation, restoration, and the triumph of love, and how it caters to our wishes to believe that intimacy and love can be enduring elements within human relationships. We turn now to the more difficult question of this particular metaphor's value for contemporary liberationist discourse. Probing into the way metaphors work, we have seen how they partially illumine some aspects of human life and profoundly distort others, how they manipulate our thinking toward certain ideals, how they reflect the social agenda of their context, and how they play upon certain emotional responses while obscuring critical distortions. We must now question in the final pages of this study what, if anything, there is to gain today from continuing to use a metaphor that elevates violence against women to a theological insight. One might argue that despite the violence against women that inheres in the metaphor, the marriage metaphor gives us a way of talking theologically about the divine–human bond and the human–human bond with language that emphasizes connectedness, intimacy, love, family, and matters of the heart. It may be possible, then, that the excessive violence of the marriage metaphor can be instructive in what it tells us about the risks of connectedness and intimacy. It certainly allows us to acknowledge those aspects of our relationship with God that remain unresolved and cannot be easily integrated into a theological tradition that emphasizes God's nature as good and all-powerful. To risk opening ourselves up to the possibility that a metaphor which imagines women's subjugation can still be useful to us in what it teaches about the dark side of love, we need first to consider our options as readers.[18]

This study has argued throughout, both explicitly and implicitly, that readers cannot hope to resist the power that religiously inspired texts of terror have over us until we understand why and how objectionable texts simultaneously fascinate and repel us as readers.[19] Until we understand how language and images play upon our fantasies, we cannot hope to begin to understand or to explain why the marriage metaphor continues to wield enormous influence over our thinking about God, about ourselves, and about what it means to be in relationship with God. To break the hold texts have over us, we must admit how much we have been shaped by them and how intricately woven throughout the fabric of our society is their vision of life.

Feminist reading theorists have called attention to the ways in which androcentric texts demand that women and other marginalized readers undermine themselves and suppress their own identities and values when reading texts by male authors.

Reading texts written by men requires women—for the sake of argument—to see women and other marginal populations as demonic, as peripheral, or as invisible. In the case of the prophetic texts that are at the center of this study, women readers are expected to indulge the brutal rape and mutilation of women in order to comprehend the ways of God. To appreciate the depth of the husband's love and compassion in reconciling with his depraved wife, one must first acquiesce to the power the husband has to dominate and penalize his wife. This can leave women readers having for the most part to read the prophets' accounts of the promiscuous wife with a bad conscience, at once attracted to and repulsed by the marital world envisioned by the authors, charmed by its promises but silenced by its assumptions.[20] Reading texts that terrorize women requires, therefore, a dual hermeneutic: one that helps a reader to resist the ways in which texts subjugate aspects of a reader's identity, and another that allows a reader to appreciate those aspects of texts that nurture and authorize them in their struggle for personhood.[21]

What I am describing here is, of course, much easier said than done. In the Bible, modern Western readers are confronted with no ordinary book. That is, the very text that readers who are committed to liberation are wont to criticize—and rightly so, for its impulses to repress, silence, annihilate, and enslave—is the same text that has in some important ways shaped our thinking about freedom and justice. The Bible has exerted enormous influence over the Western imagination in that it stands as the single most inspiring text behind the founding of the American democratic society, embodying for us our highest ideals of what faith, hope, work, self-determination, and endurance entail. Indeed, it has provided for many of us as Western readers our strongest language for what a free and just society for all can possibly look like.[22] Women readers in America therefore find themselves in a baffling predicament as readers and critics: the text that imagines their rape and mutilation as women is also the text that advocates their noblest ideals as citizens and as human beings.

All of this only underscores the fact that reading is not the passive, private, neutral experience that we have previously believed. To read is to be prepared in many respects to fight defensively. It is to be prepared to resist, to avoid, to maneuver around some of the counterproductive impulses within the text. In short, reading does not mean simply surrendering oneself totally to the literary strategies and imaginative worlds of narrators. It also means at the very least that one must be conscious of the ways in which symbolic speech, for example, draws us into its designs and attempts to mold our beliefs and identity. Metaphors, as we have seen, accomplish this by exploiting associations, by drawing connections where there were none before, by organizing and reorganizing our experiences of reality, and by accentuating some attributes while ignoring others. In the case of the story of the promiscuous wife, what happens is that women, on the one hand, are typecast as loose, shameless, erratic, and not to be trusted. Men, on the other hand, are seen as loving, generous, passionate, and forgiving. In the end, not only are all the attributes and emotions associated with sexually promiscuous women imputed to Israel. More dangerously, all the attributes associated with the deity are conferred upon husbands. If the metaphor is read uncritically, women find themselves casually accepting the ways in which they are demonized and victimized, and husbands begin demanding the authority and reverence generally reserved for deities.

It should be acknowledged that behind this study of biblical metaphors is the belief that all literature, even "inspired literature," is created. Behind its seemingly smooth, perfectly wrought frame was an author who agonized over his subject matter, who painstakingly shaped the language and crafted each phrase, who argued with himself about the direction in which to take the work, who made a decision about the best strategy to make the work do what he wanted it to do, only to change his mind when things began to fall apart and begin anew. At every turn in the prophets' speeches the authors made use of some literary devices that they believed would make their works intelligible, interesting, and rewarding to an imaginary reader.

A work that bears and invites reading, rereading, and future readings for years to come is one in which the author has succeeded in at least two things. First, the author has succeeded in masking in great part the sweaty internal fight the author had within himself or herself of choosing, abandoning, and employing different techniques. So controlled, detached, and unwavering must the author, or, in our case, the prophet's voice, be that it comes across as natural and unwavering to its audience. The author's primary objective is to hide the mechanisms that went into producing the work. The language must not sweat, the seams must not show, and the author's anguish about it all must be concealed. We have observed how the prophets Hosea, Jeremiah, and Ezekiel exploited the stereotypes associated with marriage and sex painstakingly to fashion their arguments so as (1) to arrest their audiences' attention; (2) to expose what they felt were their audiences' patently false reasonings; and (3) to build upon the androcentric interests and power relations cherished by their male audience to rationalize divine judgment. One can almost imagine the prophets standing in the squares or at the temple gates spouting their warnings, pleas, and denunciations with seeming confidence and polish to audiences unsuspecting of the prophets' internal anguish over the most effective way to win their audiences.[23]

A second way in which an author succeeds in creating a work that bears reading and rereading is when he or she is able to fashion for audience and author alike a "shareable imaginative world."[24] It is a world made up of the literary decisions the author has made, the social assumptions with which the author operates, and the vision the author proposes as sublime—all of which, the author insists, are worth the audience's submission.

Finding ways, as I have advocated, to step outside the reading process and to break the hold the prophets' writings have on us should not be viewed as a call for readers to rise up against the writers of the Bible and reject everything they have written, renouncing their every rhetorical move, questioning their every motive, alert to their every literary ploy.[25] What is needed, rather, are ways of reading the Bible that empower readers to question writers, that help them to recognize the choices writers make in shaping their message, and that allow readers to weigh the vision that writers offer. Reading the Bible should be no less a lively conversation between writer and reader than is reading other pieces of literature. Readers should have the right to question which visions offered by the Bible's writers are worth devoting one's energies to implementing in the world. Those visions readers decide are not worth inhabiting—that is, the ones that call for slaughtering and silencing others—should be critiqued and resisted.

Reading the Bible in ways it wasn't meant to be read does not mean that one is always and automatically able to resist the influence its content has exerted on readers. Reading is a far more complex process than this discussion can fully elucidate. Moreover, the reason why readers are drawn to some texts and not others, why they identify with certain characters while completely ignoring others, why some texts elicit a second, third, fourth, and repeated rereading and succeed in lingering in readers' minds years after they were read, while other texts are totally forgettable, is connected to the authors' skills and insight. What makes a text a memorable one for a reader has also to do with a reader's individual tastes, preferences, background, and the context in which the reader reads (e.g., scholarly guild, fundamentalist church group, literature class, seminary).

Great authors need great readers—readers who make demands upon their authors. Great readers, on the one hand, push authors to envision (literary) worlds that are worth the readers' efforts to inhabit—if only for the amount of time it takes to finish reading the work. (Truly great books leave readers changed by the author's vision and inspired to help bring about the world the author envisions.) Great writers, on the other hand, anticipate the questions great readers invariably pose to them such as, Why should I leave the world I currently live in and surrender myself to the imaginary world created here in this work? How does the vision in this work improve on the world as I now experience it? Who benefits and who loses from a world like this? Reading texts such as the ones in the prophetic corpus that sensationalize violence against women requires readers to find out how, if at all, violence—even in the form of divine punishment—improves the world. Readers have the responsibility to examine the ways in which they are being tempted by writers to read against their own interests. When women—even for the sake of argument—are mutilated by and in religious texts, how has the kingdom of God with its promise of peace, justice, righteousness, and love been made more authentic within the world? Whatever gain there is in continuing to use the marriage metaphor, therefore, should be based at least in part on its ability to help readers perceive themselves, God, and the world in ways that make violence and abuse intelligible, if that is possible. However provocative, enthralling, and entertaining a work may be, readers have the right to reject living in worlds that in the end diminish their humanity.

A Metaphor Gone Awry

We have seen in previous chapters that one of the important gains of the marriage metaphor is its potential to offer us an organic model of human existence. By weaving together three discourses—the religious, the political, and the social—the marriage metaphor illustrates the ways in which our religious, political, and social actions cohere with and impact one another.

Whether or not we agree with the way the metaphor condemns adulterous wives and leaves the adultery of husbands completely unexamined, the metaphor declares ultimately that our moral decisions have social, environmental, and global consequences. It offers us a way to view soberly the extent to which we have wounded the world. It does this by rejecting any false distinctions that might be made between the private, domestic world of women and the public, divinely invested world of men. Sex and politics are the same, ideologically speaking, according to the marriage metaphor. That is, all of human life coheres, and the decisions made in one sphere of our lives will eventually be felt in the other spheres of our lives. According to the prophet Hosea, the spheres affected by our (private) decisions are frequently ones we never imagined or intended.

For instance, promiscuity (idolatry) was cause for an ecological crisis that threatened to make the land dry, parched, and uninhabitable (Hos 2:3, 12). Indeed, reconciliation between God/husband and Israel/wife would reestablish the ecological balance (Hos 3:16–20), restoring stability simultaneously in the family, society, and the environment (Hos 3:21–23). Although it is lamentable that women's bodies are brutalized and their positions in society are circumscribed in order to make the point, the metaphor ultimately forces its audience to see that every decision made, whether in the public or private realm, has communal consequences.

But despite its gains as an organic model reminding us of the interconnectedness of life, and despite its capability to offer intimacy, love, and family as theological concepts, somewhere the marriage metaphor goes horribly awry. To the extent that the metaphor is used by the prophets to rationalize and explain the destruction and demise of a nation, violence, retribution, and punishment became unavoidable aspects of the metaphor. For ancient audiences, the metaphor connoted power and authority, and its promises of reconciliation and grace were secondary themes. It ties love and intimacy to aggression, power, domination, and authority; and it makes women's bodies and sexuality the object of male abuse and control.

In view of our generation's effort to grapple with our appetite for violence, given our attempts to curb the rampant violence within our culture and the violent impulses within our own heart, and as long as women continue to be the victims of some of the most depraved and brutal impulses of violence in our society, then the metaphor of battered wife is admittedly a very risky trope to use to help shed light on questions of God's response to human failures. There is nothing compelling about the prophets' vision: Why should I as reader leave the world where I presently live, where violence against wives is unjustifiable, to inhabit a world where violence against wives is taken for granted? The marriage metaphor is useless therefore for shedding light on the theological question of punishment and judgment. In other words, there is, as far as this writer is concerned, no similarity between battering husbands and avenging gods.[26]

For modern audiences, then, as long as the metaphor's principle concern is to reinforce notions of hierarchy, power, and retribution, it is a problematic device for those of us committed to the work of mending the broken places in our generation and healing the damage done within our culture. If metaphors are what we live by, and if they help us to imagine who God is, then we run the risk of making ourselves into the image of the deity who threatens, mutilates, and destroys.

Metaphors Hurt

If there were doubts before, there should be none any longer that metaphors matter. Metaphors help to shape our understanding of reality by emphasizing some things over others, by organizing our way of thinking about things in ways we had not before. They help us to see ourselves and each other and to respond to what we see in ourselves and in others in new (sometimes unintended) ways. Metaphors matter because they are sometimes our first lessons in prejudice, bigotry, stereotyping, and in marginalizing others—even if only in our minds. They deserve our scrutiny because they are intrinsic to the way we live and shape reality. We are bombarded regularly with examples in literature (e.g., novels, newspapers, magazines, advertising labels) and in the media (e.g., commercial jingles, religious music, billboards, bumper stickers) of the subtle ways in which metaphors, pithy sayings, playful ditties, and puns seep into our subconscious and arrest our imagination. Before we know it, in the innocent act of singing favorite tunes, recounting jokes, and praying prayers, we can be advocating our demise and the demise of everything and everyone dear to us—and not even know it. To illustrate the point, let me use an analogy, itself metaphorical but relevant.

Let us imagine this. A seven-year-old African American child is escorted by his mother to the front of the church for his first public speech. The young boy is nervous but has been taught to take pride in the occasion. It is February, African American History Month, and the tiny black church he attends is celebrating the history and survival of American people of African descent. This Sunday afternoon the adults are passing on to the youth rituals and traditions dear to the survival of African American people. The room is quiet, and the child's mother nods her head, signaling to him that he should begin his speech. Imagining, as his father had suggested, that the room was filled with all of his favorite stuffed animals instead of the adults and friends that make up the tiny church, the young boy swallows the lump in his throat and begins reciting Psalm 137.

> By the rivers of Babylon—
> > there we sat down and there we wept
> > when we remembered Zion.

> On the willows there
>> we hung up our harps.
> For there our captors
>> asked us for songs,
> and our tormentors asked for mirth, saying,
> "Sing us one of the songs of Zion!"

For reasons only they understand, this ode to rivers, remembering, captivity, and Zion makes old women with petal hats close their eyes and rock back and forth while old men with big handkerchiefs wipe their eyes. His mother and father smile in his direction. For reasons they do not yet understand, even the boy's friends sit spellbound. The words to this favorite psalm grip the collective memory of the little black church.

> "How could we sing the LORD's song
> in a foreign land?"

The child repeats this line for effect. With each line, his voice grows stronger, his confidence increases until he can't remember why he was first afraid; he is buoyed by the pride on everyone's face, and his voice crescendoes with confidence and conceit as he comes to the closing lines of the psalm. He speaks slowly for the effect, repeating the lines the way he had done a thousand times in his head:

> O daughter Babylon, you devastator!
>> Happy shall they be who pay you back
>> what you have done to us!
> Happy shall they be who take your little ones
>> and dash them against the rock!

A stunned silence greets the final lines. No one speaks. Awe is replaced with embarrassment on the adult faces. The boy's parents stare at each other in puzzlement. His friends return to their games in the back row, unaware of the stir about them. Several people in the audience look down at the page in their Bibles. It seems that no one recalled ever seeing those lines attached to the end of Psalm 137. No one remembers ever hearing them recited aloud. Perhaps they have, but they certainly have never heard them on a child's lips. On a child's lips, the demand to kill other children sounds obscene. The young boy steps down from the pulpit, not sure what to make of the stir in the room. It is not until he has walked all the way back to the last row to join his friends that someone remembers to clap.

This story, like many stories in the Bible, perhaps never happened, but invariably always happens. For one thing, it dramatizes for us the dilemma of terrifying texts. It also dramatizes, in ways scholarly discourse can never explicate, how authors, readers, texts, and reading contexts intersect with one another in a drama frequently filled with tension and contemplation. Contexts shape readings, and readers respond differently to texts. There are reasons why the adults in the congregation had for all their adult life virtually ignored the last two verses of Psalm 137, and there are reasons why they heard those verses that Sunday afternoon in a way they had never heard them before. There are reasons why the young boy was drawn to those verses that Sunday afternoon, and reasons why he and his friends were oblivious to the verses' implications for them as young readers. There are reasons why the sight and sound of a young child instigating the brutal death of other young children was startling and astounding on the lips of a child.

Metaphors matter, finally, because they teach us how to imagine what has previously remained unimaginable. In this case, the battered, promiscuous wife in the books of Hosea, Jeremiah, and Ezekiel makes rape, mutilation, and sexual humiliation defensible forms of retaliating against wives accused of sexual infidelity. Audiences are invited to imagine with the writers plausible ways of treating women; they are persuaded to believe that

violence against others can be ennobling to one's damaged reputation and that a marriage based on fear and humility is a
respectable way to live with one's intimate mate. Combined with
the spate of stories found throughout scripture of women's subjugation and humiliation the marriage metaphor makes violence against women not simply inevitable but theologically
defensible. Before the metaphor made its way into religious discourse, violence against wives may have been prevalent but it is
doubtful that it was attributable to God.

As we have seen, metaphors need not be accurate to capture
the imagination, nor do they need to present matters from all
angles to be convincing. They merely need to play upon stereotypes and capitalize on deeply felt emotions to be compelling. A
metaphor that takes for granted violence in the home should not
only matter to us; it should haunt us. We ought to be disturbed
by the thought that it is possible and imaginable for us to hurt,
maim, and kill those whom we say we love.

Reading texts that rationalize violence, that eroticize violence,
and that take for granted one group's power to destroy another
should never be taken lightly. What the story of our hypothetical
child speaker teaches us is that if we are not careful we may be
plotting our own demise and not even know it. Readers are
affected by what they read. Metaphors can hurt. Metaphors can
distort. Metaphors can kill. Metaphors can oppress. In this study
of the marriage metaphor, the attempt has been made to show
the potential of metaphors also to liberate, to inspire, to galva-
nize, and to give us access to one another's deeply felt but inarticulable feelings.

Metaphors as Pointing Fingers

In the field of biblical studies we have barely known how to
inquire into the figurative nature of biblical language. But with
the help of newer methodological approaches, we are able to

press beyond mere interpretation to criticism, to attempt, as
much as possible, to step outside the sublime ideology of the
text, to understand where the text gets its power and to find ways
to challenge as much as possible the power it has over us. Our
criticism does not intend to destroy the Bible, as though that
were possible (and whatever that means). Rather, it is to help
those of us interested in reading and interpreting the Bible to
find ethical ways to read intelligibly and responsibly. Indeed,
even those of us who have devoted our lives to analyzing the
Bible and searching for ways to resist its distortions, by our very
preoccupation with this document, show that we too remain
inescapably under its influence and are unable to shake completely its hold over our thinking. However obscene may be its
portrayal of women—and there are some scenes that are unbear-
ably obscene—the metaphor of Israel as promiscuous wife does
denounce many of the injustices that are of concern to those
committed to liberation: abuses by the ruling elite, political
greed, moral decay, social disintegration, and imperialist policies. Yet even those committed to liberation are still unable to
explain why, in view of the Bible's parochialism, androcentri-
cism, and colonial worldviews, many of us cannot simply ignore
it and create for ourselves an alternative canon that would more
accurately and justly represent our scientific, moral, and social
outlook. It may be because, despite its dubious origin, despite its
attempts to hide the strategies that produced it, despite our dissatisfaction with the language and perspective it uses to describe
itself, we still find gripping the glimpses of peace, justice, and
love it offers readers, however flawed and fleeting they might be.
Just as miraculous as it may seem that love can be restored in a
relationship once ripped apart by betrayal and violence, equally
spellbinding is the possibility that there is a kingdom where
good news is preached to the poor (Isa 61:1; cf. Luke 4:18),
where the last are first, where swords are permanently transformed into plowshares (Micah 4:3), where justice rolls down

like water (Amos 5:24), and where knowledge of God is unmediated by texts and human beings but is carved into the hearts of every person (Jer 31:34).

Biblical language and imagery pose serious problems when they cease to be metaphorical speech, a finger pointing beyond itself, and become the finger itself. Along with perceiving a thread of similarity between two otherwise dissimilar objects, thinking metaphorically also entails holding in tension with one another the similarity and dissimilarity, the "is" and the "is not-ness" of the signifier and the thing signified.[27] Problems arise when the metaphor "succeeds," meaning that the reader becomes so engrossed in the pathos and the details of the metaphor that the *dissimilarities* between the two are disregarded. When that happens, as Sallie McFague has pointed out, God is no longer *like* a husband, God *is* a husband: the thing signified *becomes* the signification itself. From there a risky metaphor gives rise to a risky deduction: in this case, to the extent that God's covenant with Israel is like a marriage between a man and a woman, and to the extent that divine retribution is theologically acceptable, the image of a husband physically retaliating against his wife becomes unavoidable. Such is the risk of metaphorical language. It is the risk of oversimplification and rigid correspondence. The danger is that the tolerability of one can be presumed and conferred upon the other. It is a risk against which we ought always to be on guard.

If we are willing, however, to sever the ties within the metaphor between the erotic and violence, between love and aggression, then the marriage metaphor might have the potential to shed light on a range of otherwise unexamined aspects of bonded love. We have seen elsewhere how the metaphor calls attention to the contractual character of the divine–human relationship, the stormy character of that relationship, the magnitude of the deity's love, the interrelatedness of life, and the fickleness of the human heart. It is time now to consider the power this metaphor has to help us confess our own brokenness and to allow us to acknowledge the ways in which we have broken God's heart as well.

A Metaphor of Brokenheartedness[28]

If as modern readers we are condemned to take metaphors as they come to us, if we have to accept the social and cultural values ancient audiences invested in their metaphors, then the metaphor of the adulterous wife will always remain useless to those of us committed to the liberation of women. But if we have the right and the responsibility to rethink the language we have inherited from the past and to reinvest that language with values and visions that will ennoble human life today, then the marriage metaphor may be helpful. It encapsulates many of the most important principles advocated by contemporary feminist theologians. For one thing, the marriage metaphor can help us turn from viewing the world through the eyes of the powerful, the dominant, and the strong. Seeing ourselves through the eyes of a woman, however defiled, depraved, incorrigible, and battered, forces us to ponder what it means to be weak, vulnerable, helpless, without voice, and oppressed. The story of her battering lets us see the ways in which we have been wounded and the ways in which we have wounded each other—in our family relations as well as in nonfamilial connections.

More importantly, seeing our relationship with God as a marriage drama may help us finally glimpse some of the ways in which we have been wounded by patriarchy; that is, the ways in which our veneration of power, might, hierarchy, domination, and violence has encouraged us to make decisions that have caused the destruction of our environment and have distorted our sense of the self in relationship to others. While feminists have proposed a number of metaphors for human and divine interrelatedness (e.g., lover, friend, companion, body), the marriage metaphor can be particularly useful to us because in it we are allowed to think with our hearts and not just with our minds. We are permitted to feel deeply about what we have done to each other and what has been done to us by one another and by patriarchal institutions. If there is, as feminists have argued, considerable healing and creativity that await us when we tap into our erotic potential—that is, the power that comes from being self-conscious of our interrelatedness, vulnerability, and openness to those around us—then contemplating our connectedness to one another as akin to a marriage bond gives us a way of coming to grips with the powerful emotions that erupt when communities with different backgrounds, beliefs, and competing visions of the ways things ought to be come together. Seeing ourselves as hopelessly wedded to one another and forcing ourselves to do the hard work of hearing each other out as we speak about the pain each has caused the other are what will build stronger relationships between us all. We need relationships strong enough to keep us together when we feel the urge to walk away because the pain that comes with repairing the damage of patriarchy is too great.

The marriage metaphor mirrors the ways we, women and men, have wounded each other and have been wounded by interactions marred by power, politics, and irrational expectations. All of this has left us deeply divided and bitter—estranged from, angry at, and suspicious of one another. For once, we might be able to admit, with the assistance of this metaphor, that part of our pain is the realization that, to our shame, hurting and being hurt have been always a part of what it has meant for us to live together as women and men.

Finally, the marriage metaphor permits us to believe in the most unbelievable of all possible responses to our woundedness, namely, grace. Perhaps the reason marriage seems to us as modern readers like such an unsuitable metaphor for talking about love and mutuality is because the statistics facing modern marriages argue against believing in unmerited forgiveness. The sordid details of failed marriages are constantly before us, making us cynical about the possibility of experiencing miracles in love. But this is precisely the possibility held out in the marriage metaphor. It insists that forgiveness and mercy are as natural to bonded love as are anger and hurt. Those whom we love we forgive; and those who love us forgive us. It is a mystery. That we risk loving again those who have wounded us, and that others trust us to try again despite the fact that we have broken their hearts—this is grace. It is a breathtaking possibility in the marriage metaphor that should humble us as readers.

Conclusion

Ultimately, this study, which examines the way a particular biblical metaphor proposes to personify divine–human relations, is also about the limits and gains of human language. By isolating and looking at marital and female sexual imagery and examining its use in prophetic literature, this study has sought to provide first an opportunity to examine the way in which the language of the prophets shocked, informed, shaped, and influenced their audiences, and the power of that language to include, exclude, silence, and maim. Second, this study has addressed questions of reading for liberation when confronted with language and imagery intended more to shock than to edify. This study insists that claims that the marital metaphor is "*only* a metaphor" and that sexual violence is "*only* a theme of the metaphor" do not insulate either one from serious theological scrutiny. Philosophers and critics of language, among whom feminists have been at the forefront, have shown repeatedly that the impact of language—and metaphors in particular—on a culture is no small thing. Metaphors remind us what is imaginable. Language influences our thinking about what is true, real, or possible. Not only does the image of the promiscuous wife have the potential to reinforce violence against women. It also has the potential to exclude whole segments of the population from hearing and responding to the biblical message. It does this by asking women who have been raped and violated or who live with the threat of rape and violation to join with writers in inhabiting a world where women's rape and violation are theologically justifiable. On these grounds alone, metaphors require our constant vigilance.

Moreover, one should admit that this study of the metaphor of the promiscuous wife is in many respects misleading. One might get the impression that figurative speech is rational, univocal, and transparent—so much so that its power can be easily scrutinized, classified, evaluated, and resisted. In fact, however, what makes a metaphor like the promiscuous wife so difficult to examine—which is precisely what makes it a powerfully gripping literary device for demagogues—is our complicated, contradictory response to the sexual drama embodied in the metaphor. Sex arouses a web of mixed emotions in modern audiences, as it no doubt did in ancient audiences. We don't know quite what to make of a story about a wife who engages in sexual relations with other men and a husband who strikes out at her in retaliation. With whom do we place our sympathies: the battered wife or the humiliated husband?[29] How are we to interpret what takes place in this drama?

Recent research in the area of the history of human sexuality has argued against the tendency to view sexual practices as having universal meaning(s). From one culture to the next and from one period to the next, a sexual act can change in what it means to audiences. For example, just a few decades ago in this country the extramarital sexual affairs of political leaders were never spoken of in polite settings beyond a whisper and would never have found their way onto the front page of any reputable newspaper in the country. There was a gentleman's agreement between press and politicians that private indulgences were off the record and irrelevant to an official's competence and character. Today, however, every aspect of a politician's life—especially his or her sexual behavior—is open to public scrutiny and media comment. In other words, the adultery of politicians has taken on a totally different meaning from what it had a few decade ago.

Because sexual practices generate a host of meanings depending on their context, interpreters must go beyond merely describing a particular act as forbidden and asking who forbade it, to whom it was forbidden, and under what circumstances it was forbidden. When we begin to see sex as having its own history of representation, many of the sexual practices alluded to, taken for granted, and hotly contended throughout the Old Testament can be more clearly understood. Thus, sexual practices such as taking foreign women in during war, having sexual relations with a king's wife or concubine, or abandoning one's concubine on the doorstep to be raped and ravaged by townsmen are not to be interpreted simply as universally recognized acts of moral depravity. Depending on the context and the period in which they took place, such acts can have profoundly different meanings. In the Old Testament scenes that involve sex, something more is frequently being contested than simply issues of morality. Often at stake are power, property, honor and prestige, purity, progeny, and definitions of masculinity. There are aspects of the marriage metaphor—details in the descriptions of the marriage, nuances in the husband's threats, aspects of her infidelity—that would have been immediately understood by ancient audiences but are lost upon modern readers.

How modern readers appropriate metaphors, some of whose cultural and theological values are no longer widely assumed, depends at least in part on whether the metaphor has ceased to be a metaphor and has become a way of conceiving and structuring reality. That is, it depends on whether the metaphor has evolved over the years to be no longer one of numerous possible ways of imaging God, but has become the model[30] for interpreting reality. It has become *the* interpretive grid through which one relates to and conceptualizes God. Although the promiscuous wife metaphor is not *the* dominant biblical metaphor (whereby one could not think or speak about God without thinking of God as a husband), it does function as an important auxiliary metaphor in as much as it reinforces what has come to be *the* dominant image for conceptualizing God—namely, that God is male. But what happens when modern audiences are no longer willing to take the maleness of God for granted as did their ancient counterparts? Are there ways to read the Bible that respect the humanity and intelligence of readers?

In modern times, with increasing numbers of women and other previously marginalized groups adding their voices to the theological debate, there has been increasing criticism of and attack against the oppressive, hierarchical, dualistic, male-dominated context of religious tradition and theological discourse. At the center of that critique has been the demand for religious traditions to broaden the parameters of theological imagining to include women, ethnic groups, classes, and intellectual partners who represent a more diverse, wide-ranging scope of human experience. Indeed, the growing number of women and other marginalized groups engaged in the academic study of religion is representative of the larger social, economic, and demographic changes taking place in the wider society. Thus, in the face of the ever-changing complexion of American society, every new generation is faced with the task of examining and criticizing the epistemological, cultural, and theological paradigms that have been handed down to it by the previous generation. In view of our growing concern about the pervasiveness of violence within our culture and our increased sensitivity to the ways in which women's sexuality is demonized in our culture, biblical language about the rape and sexual humiliation of wives may be, to paraphrase Abraham Heschel, an octave too high for the modern heart to contemplate matters of justice, retribution, and power.[31]

Thanks to Israel's ancient poets, prophets, and rhetoricians, we have a wealth of biblical metaphors at our disposal to help us understand our relationship with God. The sheer range of these metaphors suggests that the ancient community was itself well aware of the limitations of human language to capture the full essence of humans' experiences with God. The audience understood that there are as many ways to speak about God and one's relationship to God as there are experiences to be lived. One finds in the Old Testament, therefore, imagery as varied as that of king–vassal, shepherd–sheep, lord–servant, woman in labor–child, judge–defendant/plaintiff, parent–child, husband–wife; and non-human images such as lion–prey, moth–cloth, and dew–lily. Each one brings with it its own fresh and unique insight. Taken alone, each limits our vision of what it means to be human and skews our understanding of what it means to be in relationship with God. But taken together, all of them make sure that no single concept becomes a false god and that we have a variety of metaphors to reflect a wide range human experiences.[32]

It is certainly true that reinterpreting marriage as a metaphor in the Bible, if that were possible, does very little to change the fact that the Bible's culture takes for granted women's limited roles and goes out of its way at times to reinforce the notion that women's sexuality poses a dangerous threat to the social order. Rethinking the Bible's representation of marriage will not change the fact that both the Bible's culture and our own culture persistently rationalize violence against women. But as often as we are confronted in the media with demagogues and myth-makers condemning women for the culture's instabilities, as often as we witness violence and never feel remorse, this project hopes to remind us that there is a difference between a pointing finger (marriage metaphor) and the object to which it points (God). The two should never be confused—despite the fact that sometimes the closest we seem to get to the object is the tip of our own finger. And even then we can't always make out precisely what we're looking at.

Notes

Introduction

1. For a brief study of the range of sex- and body-related imagery in all the prophetic books where it occurs, see David J. Clark, "Sex-Related Imagery in the Prophets," *The Bible Translator* 33 (1982): 409–13.

2. This is not to say that marriage was seen as, nor was in actuality, a totally negative experience for women or for men. There were certainly women whose marriages diverged from the norm, women who enjoyed their own sphere of influence (if not power), and women who did not think of themselves as subjugated (and men who didn't think of themselves as "over" their wives). Nevertheless, it cannot be denied that Hebrew laws (and narratives) overwhelmingly benefited men and supported androcentric interests. Women had hardly any redress, for instance, should they find themselves in situations with neglectful, abusive husbands.

3. Adultery carried with it a penalty of death for both partners (Deut 22:22), to be sure, but a man who raped an unengaged virgin could get away with paying her father for despoiling the latter's property (22:28–29). Moreover, the priests came up with bizarre concoctions to test a husband's suspicions about his wife's fidelity (Numbers 5). No mention is made in any of the codes of any similar measures devised to test wives' suspicions about their husbands' fidelity.

4. I will not attempt to cite these works at this point. Many of them will be referenced throughout this project for the various insights they

lend to my own work. But for classic works by feminists on the way the Bible represents women, see the two exemplary works by Phyllis Trible, *God and the Rhetoric of Sexuality* (Philadelphia: Fortress, 1978) and *Texts of Terror* (Philadelphia: Fortress, 1984); two impressive studies sponsored by the Society of Biblical Literature are *The Bible and Feminist Hermeneutics*, edited by Mary Ann Tolbert (*Semeia;* Chico, Calif.: Scholars Press, 1983), and *Feminist Perspectives on Biblical Scholarship*, edited by Adela Yarbro Collins (SBL Centennial Publications 10; Chico, Calif.: Scholars Press, 1985). One of the earliest and classic discussions of the importance of language deconstruction for feminist criticism is found in the introduction to *Womanspirit Rising: A Feminist Reader in Religion,* edited by Carol P. Christ and Judith Plaskow (New York: Harper & Row, 1979).

5. Representation theorists have argued convincingly that the act of representing involves two concurrent and related gestures: characterizing an object and articulating the subject's judgment. This means that we have in prophetic rhetoric not women's construction of their own subjectivity but men's interpretations of women's reality. Hence, from the characterizations of women as harlots, widows, and barren women to the legal prescriptions having to do with purity, rape, and divorce, and from the narratives extolling the virtues of exceptional women to, at last, the descriptions of the lewd promiscuous woman in prophetic rhetoric, what we have in biblical literature is female sexuality interpreted by biblical men. Indeed, the sexual experiences of biblical women have been replaced by men's interpretations of what it means to be female. In this case, we have the prophets' interpretations of the female body, their perceptions of women's sexuality, and their definitions of how decent women should behave. This means, of course, that we know more about what ancient Israelite prophets thought about women than about the women themselves.

6. The only possible exception to this may be the contents of the Song of Songs. The female experiences, thoughts, imaginations, emotions, and words expressed in Song of Songs are so central to the book's unfolding, and the amount of space attributed to female speakers is so striking that it is not difficult to imagine that a woman was the author of this stirring meditation on female longing.

7. I am well aware there are some who deny that it is possible to do both. We cannot both affirm and critique the biblical universe, they

argue, without reinscribing the dualisms patriarchy espouses. Moreover, by trying to hold in tandem both the emancipatory and subjugating elements in biblical texts, we remain naïve to the complex ways in which sexism, classism, colonialism, racism, and body politics are intricately interstructured in patriarchal cultures. Biblical texts are not more or less oppressive; interpreters cannot excise the oppressive impulses in the Bible and retain its liberating practices.

I am equally well aware that there are some stories in the Bible narrating women's mutilation where the only sane option is to judge the story hopelessly irredeemable.

The point here is that to the extent that metaphors represent methodical, deliberate, shrewd attempts by mythmakers to mask a society's contradictions and to divert attention away from the gaps in its thinking, then the task of the exegete, it seems to me, is to help readers begin to read the Bible in ways the texts were not intended to be read. As long as there are women and men who still read the Bible for its theo-ethical value and have found in its pages the impetus and courage to resist oppression, then there remains—for those of us who care to do so—the responsibility to help contemporary readers to read the Bible with a suspicious hope, careful of the Bible's distortions and mindful of its possibilities.

8. One of the most widely noted critical thinkers about the archeology and power of historically situated discourse in the shaping of culture, thinking, and relationships between the possessed and dispossessed is Michel Foucault: *The Archeology of Knowledge* (New York: Harper & Row, 1972); *Power/Knowledge: Selected Interviews and Other Writings, 1972-1977*, edited by Colin Gordon (New York: Pantheon Books, 1980).

Chapter 1: "You Have the Forehead of a Whore"
The Rhetoric of a Metaphor

1. Indeed, the command to marry a promiscuous wife sets the first three chapters of Hosea in content and drama apart from the rest of scripture. This study will focus on 2:4–23 because, sandwiched as it is between two extended narrative accounts of that marriage (chaps. 1 and 3), this unit poetically characterizes the detail of that marriage in ways that make it stylistically comparable to its characterization in Jeremiah and Ezekiel.

2. Evidently the prophet Ezekiel was so gifted in his use of figurative

language that his preaching took on the drama of a performance where audiences came out specifically to hear his grandiloquent rantings (Ezek 33:30–33).

3. We see in the story of Queen Vashti how the queen's refusal of the king's request to come and display her beauty was interpreted by the pundits of the day. It represented a threat to the balance of power in the domestic realm. She was quickly deposed as queen because, according to the pundits, should word spread that the queen had defied the king, her defiance might be a model of female behavior that would threaten the security of every patriarchal household (Esth 1:13–22).

4. This feeling of linguistic estrangement from the Holy Other was captured by Israel's poets, for example, Second Isaiah: "To whom will you liken God, / or what likeness compare with God?" (Isa 40:18).

5. Indeed, according to the prophet Hosea (12:10), God specifically speaks to prophets in parables (Hebrew *dimmâ*) The word translated "speak in parables" (RSV) is derived from the same Hebrew root as the word for "likeness" in Gen 1:26. Interestingly, the NRSV editors chose to ignore the parallelism with *ḥāzôn* in the adjoining stich in Hos 12:10 and read the root *dmh* instead as "to end, destroy, cease"; hence their translation: ". . . and through the prophets I will bring destruction."

6. George Caird, *The Language and Imagery of the Bible* (Philadelphia: Westminster; London: Duckworth, 1980), 177.

7. Sallie McFague, *Metaphorical Theology: Models of God in Religious Language* (Philadelphia: Fortress, 1982), 15.

8. This term is borrowed from Tikva Frymer-Kensky's discussion of what she calls the metaphor of the "wanton wife of God." See her fine study of the development of gender roles and imagery in the ancient Israelite culture: *In the Wake of the Goddess: Women, Culture, and the Biblical Transformation of Pagan Myth* (New York: Free Press, 1992).

9. Nowhere in Hebrew law are husbands actually granted the right to retaliate physically against their wives. But, given the enormous power husbands had over their wives, the fact that women had hardly any arena for legal redress for their grievances against their husbands (compare the rituals established for redressing husbands' suspicions of their wives' infidelity in Numbers 5), and in light of our growing knowledge of the pervasive nature of domestic violence, it is probably safe to assume that Hebrew wives were victims of physical battery and other

punitive actions by their husbands more often than anyone in the elite, literate circles that produced the Bible cared to acknowledge.

10. Not only do the scribes throughout the psalms rejoice in God's power and might; they also imagine Israel and its king to be the praise and envy of their neighbors, who recognize them as uniquely favored by Yahweh (Psalms 66, 67, 87, 105). This is certainly part of Ezekiel's argument in his use of the marriage metaphor, when he comments on the fame and renown the woman enjoyed in the beginning when she became her husband's wife (Ezek 16:13–14).

11. See Hosea's use of the metaphor in chap. 11.

12. The idea of a tender relationship between God and God's child Israel, a loving though anguished relationship, seems to be an image unique to Hosea's manipulation of the parental metaphor (Hos 11:8): "How can I give you up, O Ephraim? / How can I hand you over, O Israel? . . . / My heart recoils within me, / my compassion grows warm and tender. . . ."

13. Max Black, *Models and Metaphor: Studies in Language and Philosophy* (Ithaca, N.Y.: Cornell University Press, 1962), 38–44. Black's actual example is "Man is a wolf," where "man" is the principal subject and "wolf" the subsidiary subject. I. A. Richards's terms "vehicle" and "tenor" amount to the same thing as Black's "principal" and "subsidiary"; see Richards, *The Philosophy of Rhetoric* (New York and London: Oxford University Press, 1965).

14. Many linguists argue that meaning actually is produced in the interaction between the two subjects, which forces the audience to consider the relationship between two otherwise distinct ideas.

15. Of course, this might not apply to those whose livelihood is derived from vines. This shows that the context in which metaphors are used makes a difference. This topic will be discussed in the next chapter.

16. Black, *Models and Metaphor,* 237.

17. Terence Fretheim, *The Suffering of God: An Old Testament Perspective* (Philadelphia: Fortress, 1984), 11.

18. Based on the allegories of Ezekiel 16 and 23, perhaps to this cycle should be added the phase of female puberty (courtship/guardianship).

19. Mary Joan Winn Leith, "The Transformation of the Woman, Israel," in *Gender and Difference in Ancient Israel*, edited by Peggy L. Day (Minneapolis: Fortress, 1989), 101.

20. More will be said about this conception in the next chapter when the attention shifts to the sociocultural context underlying such constructions.

21. According to Hosea, Israel was as rebellious and disloyal as God was firm and compassionate. It is interesting to note that in Hosea 11 the gender of the parent is never identified, though commentators frequently assume that the parent (God) is male. But there is no compelling reason in the language and imagery to assume that the parent is male, and there are a number of things that argue that God is being imaged in this passage as a mother and not as a father. It is more frequently the responsibility of the mother to teach a child to walk (v. 3a), to nurse a child back to health (v. 3b), to steer a child emotionally through life (v. 4a), and to feed a child (v. 4b).

Nevertheless, while the gender of the parent in Hosea 11 may be ambiguous, there is no mistaking the motherhood of God in the writings of Second Isaiah (42:14; 46:3-4; 49:15). For more discussion on the topic, see Phyllis Trible, *God and the Rhetoric of Sexuality* (Philadelphia: Fortress, 1978), 31-71; M. Gruber, "The Motherhood of God in Second Isaiah," *RB* 90 (1983): 351-59; and John J. Schmitt, "The Motherhood of God and Zion as Mother," *RB* 92 (1985): 557-69.

22. This is true not only in poetry but also in narrative material.

23. See Clark, "Sex-Related Imagery in the Prophets," 410. According to Clark, the next three categories are nakedness/exposure, widowhood, and menstruation.

24. The poet in Isa 54:5-8 makes clear the contrasting sides of the husband's love—one moment abandoning his wife and the next embracing her; one moment wrathful and the next pardoning:

> For your Maker is your husband,
> > the LORD of hosts is his name;
> . . . .
> For the LORD has called you
> > like a wife forsaken and grieved in spirit,
> like the wife of a man's youth when she is cast off,
> > > says your God.
> For a brief moment I abandoned you,
> > but with great compassion I will gather you.
> In overflowing wrath for a moment
> > I hid my face from you;

> but with everlasting love I will have
> compassion on you,
>> says YHWH, your Redeemer.

25. It is interesting to note the ways in which the prophet Jeremiah uses both male and female animal sexual behavior to allegorize idolatry. At one point the prophet uses the image of the overly endowed lusty stallion neighing after its neighbor's mate to characterize presumably Israelite men involved in what may have been sexual relations with (cult) prostitutes (5:8). At another point he employs the image of a female camel in heat who is unrestrained in and gripped by her lust (2:23–24) to allegorize those who become defiled by idolatry.

Chapter 2: "Is She Not My Wife?"
Prophets, Audiences, and Expectations

1. Rejection, prophetic conflict, and tension with audiences are characteristic themes in prophetic literature beginning with the story of Moses and continuing into the stories of exilic and postexilic prophets such as Jeremiah and Ezekiel. These themes are so prevalent that questions have been raised whether stories about prophets clashing with audiences were conventionally included in a prophet's biography to authenticate the prophet and to shield him against charges of false prophecy (see Kathleen M. O'Connor, *The Confessions of Jeremiah: Their Interpretation and Role in Chapters 1-25* [SBLDS 94; Atlanta: Scholars Press, 1988]).

2. There have been, of course, volumes of comparative work done on the relationship between Mari prophecy and Old Testament prophecy. The bulk of this work has concerned itself with using the Mari texts to help shed light on the origins of prophecy (e.g., guilds, mysticism), the institutional setting of prophecy (e.g., cult, temple, palace), and patterns of prophetic speech (oracles of salvation, oracles of judgment). Patterns of speech have been studied largely to see how institutional context shapes genres (e.g., form criticism). There has been little interest in patterns of speech for what they might tell us about the social profile of the prophet's audience.

3. This is what structuralists mean when they speak of readers having "literary or linguistic competence." They mean that reading entails more than understanding words; it also entails being knowledgeable about the

conventions governing the use of those words in speaking or writing, aware of the rules governing the language itself, aware of what is permissible and what is impermissible in speech (see John Barton, "'Literary Competence' and Genre Recognition," in *Reading the Old Testament: Method in Biblical Study* [Philadelphia: Westminster, 1984], 11–12).

4. Many questions have been raised in recent years about the term "prophets" and whether we can talk intelligibly and soundly about actual "prophets." Serious doubts have been expressed about whether the historical prophets had anything to do with the books in the Old Testament that carry their names (see Robert Carroll, *From Chaos to Covenant: Prophecy in the Book of Jeremiah* [New York: Crossroad, 1981]; idem, "Inventing the Prophets," *IBS* 10 [1988]: 24–36). A. G. Auld argues for the late origin of the label "prophet" for the biblical prophets ("Prophets through the Looking Glass: Between Writings and Moses," *JSOT* 27 [1983]: 3–23).

5. Because writing was a very late stage in the transmission of so much of the material in the Old Testament, including the prophetic material, the term "reader(s)" may seem an inappropriate term to apply to those who first received the prophets' speeches. "Audience" sounds more suitable for our purposes. Whenever I speak about "audiences"—or "readers," for that matter—I am using the terms heuristically for the ideal receivers of the contents of the prophetic books as we now have them.

6. In this chapter I will be building upon a cross-section of methodological insights (e.g., literary criticism, deconstructionism, gender and sex studies, psychoanalytic studies) to reconstruct authors' and audiences' shared expectations and assumptions. Reader-oriented theories in particular have been helpful in providing to the biblical field insights into and tools for studying the way authors, readers, and texts interact with one another at times in surprising and unpredictable ways to generate new, unexpected meanings and consequences for understanding the Bible. For a collection of some widely cited reader-oriented essays, see *The Reader in the Text: Essays on Audience and Interpretation*, edited by Susan R. Suleiman and Inge Crosman (Princeton: Princeton University Press, 1980).

7. For just a sampling of the kinds of new questions being posed persistently to Old Testament texts, see two recent volumes, *Gender, Power, & Promise: The Subject of the Bible's First Story,* edited by Danna Nolan Fewell and David M. Gunn (Nashville: Abingdon, 1993) and *The New*

Literary Criticism and the Hebrew Bible, edited by J. Cheryl Exum and David J. A. Clines (Valley Forge, Penn.: Trinity Press International, 1993).

8. One could argue that, while form criticism emerged as a strategy for exploring the literary remains of the ancient past, Old Testament scholars applied its principles in order to penetrate beyond the literature to the ancient social settings that perpetuated conventional patterns of discourse. Newer literary-critical approaches share a similar interest in conventional patterns of speech, but not in order to analyze the ways in which institutional interests become codified in speech. Their interest, which this book shares, is in the ways in which social and moral values are codified and reinforced in the speech patterns.

9. Of course, one's intended audience and one's actual audience do not always wind up being the same audience. Sometimes prophets misjudge audiences; sometimes audiences fail to live up to prophets' expectations; sometimes audiences *refuse* to live up to prophets' expectations; and sometimes speeches fall into the hands of the wrong audience altogether. Therefore, the only audience we can speak credibly about today is the one we can infer from the choice of language and the codes of values that make up prophetic speeches. Although this audience may not be the actual audience the prophets had in mind, nor one of the earlier audiences the editors had in mind, to the extent that this audience finds the prophets' messages meaningful, it is an audience imaginable given the final shape of the book.

10. Indeed, not all men in Israel shared the metaphor's fantasies and fears about women's bodies. One can imagine that some men were probably completely turned off by the imagery and found it obscene, ludicrous, and nonsensical. But that does not negate the fact that men on the whole benefited from the metaphor's construction of male power and female powerlessness.

11. Nowhere else in scripture is comparable attention paid to the male body, seeing in it the potential for conveying theological insight about God.

One of the most exciting recent studies applying gender criticism and psychoanalytic re-readings to biblical literature is Howard Eilberg-Schwartz's study of male god-talk in Old Testament and Jewish writings. Although Eilberg-Schwartz's study came to my attention during the final stages of this study, I find absolutely fascinating his conclusion that the marriage metaphor was deliberately devised in order to

avoid the homoerotic implications of using masculine imagery to talk
about God. Imagining themselves intimately and erotically attached to
and loving a male God (as the first commandment directs) created anxiety for scribes, priests, and prophets. This caused them to metaphorize
Israel (and Hebrew men) as female to avoid the homoerotic implications of men talking about loving a male god. See Eilberg-Schwartz,
God's Phallus: And Other Problems for Men and Monotheism (Boston:
Beacon Press, 1994).

12. Julie Galambush, in her study of Ezekiel's use of the marriage
metaphor, is one of the few scholars to discuss in detail the notion that
the extravagantly lewd abuse the woman suffers in Ezekiel 16 and 23 is
pornographic and voyeuristic (*Jerusalem in the Book of Ezekiel: The City
as Yahweh's Wife* [SBLDS 130; Atlanta: Scholars Press, 1992]). As inspec-
tor of the temple and of Jerusalem, Ezekiel, says Galambush, uses the
metaphor to "'demystify' the threateningly mysterious woman, first by
investigating and exposing her secrets, and then by punishing and thus
'saving' her" (p. 161).

13. The metaphor of the promiscuous wife was not intended to give
an accurate portrait of a real life/wife situation. That is, the focus on
female infidelity, female impurity, and the rape of women was not
intended to give an accurate description of the behavior and predilec-
tions of real Hebrew women. Rather, it was a device used to play upon
the fantasies and fears of their male audiences about women. Metaphors derive their power from the intensity of feelings that stereotypes
evoke. The ways and actions of wives have been stereotyped in this
metaphor, and the behavior of adulterous wives has been exaggerated.
In the end, however, the promiscuous wife is fictional, and she is
expendable—because the metaphor was never a comment on the plight
of women; it is about the actions of men.

14. Phyllis Bird paraphrases the drama in another way: "By appealing
to the common stereotypes and interests of a primarily male audience,
[Hosea] turns their accusation against them . . . [and] says, "You (male
Israel) are that woman!" ("'To Play the Harlot': An Inquiry into an Old
Testament Metaphor," in *Gender and Difference in Ancient Israel,* edited
by Peggy L. Day [Minneapolis: Fortress, 1989], 89). No wonder the
prophets repeatedly found themselves embroiled in conflicts with their
audiences and constantly subject to danger. Unfortunately, most of
what we know about those conflicts is told from the prophets' perspec-

tives, leaving us in the dark about exactly how audiences defended themselves against the prophets' messages.

15. For a discussion of the ways in which sex and power cohere in other parts of the Bible, especially in the stories about King David, undermining the neat public and private strategies of the narrative, see Regina Schwartz, "Adultery in the House of David: The Metanarrative of Biblical Scholarship and the Narratives of the Bible," *Semeia* 54 (1991): 35–55.

16. For an excellent analysis, using the insights of narratology and anthropology, of the way sexuality, gender codes, and prestige systems are configured particularly in the Deuteronomistic Historian's narratives, see Ken Stone, "Sexual Power and Political Prestige: The Case of the Disputed Concubines," *BR* 10 (1994): 28f. This work is part of Stone's dissertation "Sex, Honor and Power in the Deuteronomistic History" (Vanderbilt University, 1995).

17. For a stark example of this kind of ideological thinking about women, see the ode to an excellent wife in Prov 31:10–31. She is lauded for her domestic chores, her charitable responsibilities and industriousness, her support of her husband, and her respect from her children. Beyond these duties, she has no other role to play.

18. Cities and locales were seen not only as wives; they were also construed as mothers (see 2 Sam 20:19; and the image of Rachel weeping for her children in Jer 31:15–17) and as daughters (e.g., the repeated references to "daughter Zion" or "daughter Jerusalem").

19. Tikva Frymer-Kensky, *In the Wake of the Goddess: Women, Culture, and the Biblical Transformation of Pagan Myth* (New York: Free Press, 1992), 172.

20. Evidently not only were capital cities compared to the beauty of women, but the compliment could be reversed by comparing a woman to the splendor and beauty of capital cities. In Israelite romance literature (Song of Songs 6:4), the vehicle and tenor reverse and the black-skinned Shulammite is compared to the beauty of the capital city of Tirzah, and her comeliness to the capital city Jerusalem.

21. See Aloysius Fitzgerald, "The Mythological Background for the Presentation of Jerusalem as Queen and False Worship as Adultery in the Old Testament," *CBQ* 34 (1972): 403–12; idem, *"Btwlt* and *Bt* as Titles for Capital Cities," *CBQ* 37 (1975): 167–83.

22. The marriage metaphor certainly embodies a number of intellectual, social, and institutional concerns that were common to the

whole of the Ancient Near East. A recent work that promises to shed some light on this topic (which was unavailable to me at the time of this writing) is *Sex and Eroticism in Mesopotamian Literature,* by Gwendolyn Leick (London: Routledge, 1994).

23. For example, in Hos 2:3ff. there is uncertainty whether the woman who will be stripped naked as the day she was born refers to the city (stripped of its inhabitants?), the land (burned and razed to the ground), or the nation (stripped of its reputation and status as a republic). Likewise, does God in 2:14ff. reconcile with the city (that is, its inhabitants—in particular the elite men who will run it), the land (hence the ecological imagery), or the nation as a whole?

24. The kinds of assumptions about shame and honor, male and female roles, and depictions of capital cities as female are the kinds of cultural information that become part of the social setting that audiences and speakers inhabit, which often remain unknown to outsiders. Some of this common heritage has been codified in Hebrew law. For example, there are laws concerning adultery, rape, and other sexual behavior in Deuteronomy 22–24 as well as the custom for handling suspected adulteresses in Num 5:1–31. All of this would have represented what Wolfgang Iser and others refer to as an "extra-textual repertoire." According to Iser, "The repertoire consists of all the familiar territory within the text. This may be in the form of references to earlier works, or to social and historical norms, or the whole culture from which the text has emerged— . . . [that is, the text's] 'extra-textual' reality" (*The Act of Reading: A Theory of Aesthetic Response* [Baltimore: Johns Hopkins University Press, 1978], 69).

25. Although the NRSV usually translates *bat Ṣiôn* as "daughter Zion," Frymer-Kensky picks up on the more poetic and sensual tones in her translation "Beloved Zion."

26. Frymer-Kensy, *In the Wake of the Goddess,* 169.

27. Because the book fails to refer directly to any specific historical events or personalities, beyond the stylized formulation of the superscription, it is difficult to date the oracles of Hosea more precisely. Francis I. Andersen and David Noel Freedman speak vaguely of the period from 740 to 730 (*Hosea: A New Translation with Introduction and Commentary* [AB 22; Garden City, N.Y.: Doubleday, 1980]). Others have placed his ministry from the mid-century down to the fall of Samaria in

721 B.C.E. (see, e.g., C. Leong Seow, "The Book of Hosea" in *Anchor Bible Dictionary* [New York: Doubleday, 1992], 3:292).

28. The northern kingdom was eventually decimated by the Assyrians in 721 B.C.E., which suggests one of three things: (1) despite Hosea's preaching, the people failed to change; (2) despite the prophet's preaching, whatever change they sought was not permanent; or (3) even if there was a change in their behavior as a result of his preaching, it came too late to avert the destruction that lay ahead.

29. Amos, who also preached to the northern kingdom during that time, was actually a native of Tekoa, a tiny village twelve miles south of Jerusalem in the southern kingdom.

30. While fragmentation of unities is characteristic of the second part of the book of Hosea (chaps. 4–14), one finds in the seeming incoherence of the narrative sequence of chaps. 1–3 an extended poem (2:1–23) bracketed on either side by two extended narrative accounts (chaps. 1 and 3). The first three chapters are biographical in style in that they center on the events surrounding the prophet's alleged marriage to a promiscuous woman. The poetic account of the marriage (2:1–23) can be compared with the imagery in the books of Jeremiah and Ezekiel.

31. The images pile up on each other here in 2:1 because the inhabitants are both children and the wife (see Hans W. Wolff, *Hosea* [Philadelphia: Fortress, 1974], 33; and James L. Mays, *Hosea* [Philadelphia: Westminister, 1969], 37). Another possibility is that the children represent the general population, the men who did not occupy positions of power and who had no say in deciding the nation's direction. And yet, like children, their fate as inhabitants was tied to the fate of the elite men who made decisions on their behalf. In other words, the commoners (men) are invited to join the prophet in protesting the abuses of the elite.

32. I depart from the NRSV in the translation of this one verse. Most commentators translate v. 2: ". . . for she is not my wife, and I am not her husband," arguing, based on parallels with Mesopotamian divorce clauses, that the expression is a formal divorce formula. Others see the expression as a satirical statement that the woman acts, for all practical purposes, *as though* they were no longer married. Nothing in the syntax prevents the expression from being taken as an interrogative, which has

the advantage of taking into account the overall shape and mood of the poem. As an interrogative, the verse sums up the basis on which the husband continues to make claims on the woman from 2:5 on.

33. Men were permitted to divorce their wives (Deut 24:1–4), although there does seem to be some attempt to protect wives from wrongful accusation or treatment (Deut 22:13–19; 22:28–29). There are no parallel laws that grant wives the right to initiate divorce from their husbands.

34. The chapter itself is testimony to the fact that physical retaliation against an adulterous wife was not unthinkable, that it was an option for a husband to take. See also chapter 2, n. 9.

35. The literature on this term is extensive; Hermann Gunkel was the first to propose that the preexilic prophets fashioned some of their denunciations against Israel in the form a formal "lawsuit" (*Gerichtsrede*), which Yahweh brought against the people. Certain elements of Gunkel's argument have since been modified, and the topic has been further illuminated by Kirsten Nielsen, *Yahweh as Prosecutor and Judge* (JSOTSup 9; Sheffield: JSOT Press, 1978), 1–26.

36. There is some speculation that the prophet is referring to pieces of clothing that were uniquely associated with prostitutes and promiscuous women. The patriarch Judah mistook his daughter-in-law Tamar for a prostitute, the text explicitly states, "for she had covered her face" (Gen 38:15). Similarly, the prophet Jeremiah, with characteristic rhetorical embellishment, accuses the woman "you have the forehead of a whore" (3:3). It is frequently the case that women who deviate from or defy social norms are compared to prostitutes.

37. The notion that nudity was problematic at best and disgraceful at worst is evident throughout material narrating the penalties for gazing at the wrong person's nakedness. Before Adam and Eve's disobedience in the garden, nakedness symbolized intimacy and stability (Gen 3:7–21). After their disobedience, humankind was clothed and their nakedness hidden. One of Noah's sons was cursed for having looked upon his father's nakedness (Gen 9:20–28). In the Holiness Code (Lev 18:6–18; 20:17–21) one finds fairly specific and comprehensive interdictions against viewing one another naked (fathers, mothers, sons, daughters, aunts, in-laws) and against incestuous relations, the inference being that one's nakedness was tied to one's sexuality, which

should be expressed only within marital relations. Nakedness is clearly threatening to stability, order, and family ties.

38. For some time scholars attempted to infer Canaanite religious practices from the prophets' use of the marriage metaphor, arguing that the metaphor reflected the prophets' polemic against Baal worship and obscene sexual practices that took place in the Canaanite cult. The allegation was that cult prostitutes and priests engaged in various orgiastic sexual rites. Scholars today are less eager to infer such practices, especially since there is no explicit evidence in either Canaanite texts or the Old Testament that any such practices ever took place. Previous generations of scholars did not consider sufficiently the rhetorical aims of the marriage metaphor to inflame emotions rather than pointing to particular sexual activity; and they underestimated the prophets' oracles of judgment as deliberate attempts at distortion and caricature. For more recent and helpful discussion of the use of *zônâ* imagery in the Old Testament, see Jo Ann Leith, "Verse and Reverse: The Transformation of the Woman, Israel, in Hosea 1-3," and "'To Play the Harlot': An Inquiry into an Old Testament Metaphor" both in *Gender and Difference in Ancient Israel*, edited by Peggy Day (Philadelphia: Fortress, 1989).

39. For more discussion of the dialogical shape of Hos 2:4-23, see my article "Gomer: Victim of Violence or Victim of Metaphor?" *Semeia* 47 (1989): 87–104.

40. One of the most persistent features of the marriage metaphor, as we will see again in Jeremiah and Ezekiel's use of it, is that it is used so broadly that it is not easy to distinguish when the prophet is inveighing against well-known political conspiracies, when against religious corruptions, and when against general moral turpitude. Unless we are to assume that each prophet was completely irreverent and iconoclastic and used sexual language solely to shock and insult his audience—which should not be ruled out completely—we can presume that the prophet's audience was quite aware of what the prophet was talking about.

41. According to the law, this was an impossibility (Deut 24:1-4; cf. Jer 2:1). Men could not reunite with women who had become sexually involved with other men.

42. Looking beyond the first three chapters of the book, one discovers that the prophet Hosea makes abundant use of poetic images to capture in various ways the nature of God's affection for and claims upon Israel

and to portray the depth of Israel's estrangement from God. Close examination of the book will show that of the fourteen or so poetic images that Hosea explores, only two are developed in any detail. The marriage metaphor is the most extensively developed and is confined to the first three chapters of the book. Next in importance is the parent–child metaphor, which emerges in the second half of the book.

43. Another literary feature of the book that intensifies its fast-paced, staccato character is the fact that chaps. 1–25 (where the marriage metaphor is found) are composed of disparate writings that seem to lack a principle of organization. In these chapters, poetry and prose commingle, and there are relatively few clues for differentiating units of material from one another (see Robert Carroll, *Jeremiah: A Commentary* [Philadelphia: Westminister, 1986]).

44. The possibility that he saw his audience as especially obtuse is made all the more probable when one considers that the prophet grappled on several occasions with the question of whether or not the people were indeed even capable of amending their ways: at times he felt that they were (3:12–13; 4:1–2), but at other times he concluded that they were not (4:22; 5:23; 13:23; 17:9).

45. For a fine summary of the way rhetorical questions are used to heighten the drama of the poetry, see Walter Brueggemann, "Jeremiah's Use of Rhetorical Questions," *JBL* 92 (1973): 358–74.

46. Although the marital imagery is confined in this unit to 2:2, it actually functions as the basis for what follows: "What wrong did your ancestors find in me, that they went far from me, and went after worthlessness, and became worthless?" (2:4)

47. See K. E. Bailey and W. L. Holladay, "'The Young Camel' and 'Wild Ass' in Jeremiah 2:23–25," *VT* (1968): 256–60.

48. The Hebrew is: *ʾêpōh lōʾ šuggalt*.

49. André Nehrer, "Le symbolisme conjugal: expression de l'histoire dan l'Ancien Testament," *RHPR* 34 (1954): 45.

50. I prefer to refer to Ezekiel 16 and 23 as "narrative metaphors" following Julie Galambush (and Paul Ricouer), instead of as "allegories" as they are commonly designated. Citing the work of literary scholars (e.g., Northrop Frye) who define an allegory as a narrative that draws a point-for-point correspondence between the allegory and its reference, each element representing something or someone else in the real world, Galambush argues that while both chaps. 16 and 23 truly have

allegorizing tendencies and elements, in fact the rich, complex interactions between tenor and vehicle that are common in metaphors miti-
gate against these chapters falling into the category of allegory. It would
be better to view them as extended metaphors because of the complex
ways in which the metaphor corresponds closely at times to the relationship between Israel and God, and at other times lapses into ·
extended diatribes against a complex range of female sexual practices,
some of which are recoverable, others not.

51. To be raped was an unbearable disgrace for a woman to endure.
Pleading with her half-brother Amnon not to rape her, Tamar reminds
him of what she would have to endure should he force her to lie with
him: "As for me, where could I carry my shame (*ḥerpātî*)?" (2 Sam
13:13). Forced sex upon virgins (but not wives?) carried severe penalties (Deut 22:22–29). To rape a betrothed woman was to jeopardize
another man's progeny. In Deut 29:29 the father is the only one mentioned as being compensated for the rape of a daughter; there does not
appear to be any concern for the woman's psychological and emotional
loss, even though to rape a woman is to violate and humiliate her emotionally and physically in the most profound of ways.

52. Perhaps we have a clue here about the social context of Ezekiel's
audience: theirs was one that questioned either God's power or God's
purposes. By the way the image is executed (e.g., first-person verbs) the
prophet insists that all power lies with the husband, whether it is to
rescue the girl-child at birth (16:1–14), to surrender her into the hands
of her so-called lovers (16:35–43: 23:22–35), or to restore her to her former dignity (16:53–63).

Speculating on the kind of religious and theological crisis triggered
by the First Deportation in 587 B.C.E., Robert Wilson proposes that the
kinds of questions that were posed for the Jerusalem royal establish-
ment, including the Zadokite priesthood of which Ezekiel was a part,
would have been questions such as: "Would the fall of the city mean
that God had been overpowered by the Babylonian deities, or had God
perhaps simply broken the eternal promise to David and rejected both
Jerusalem and Israel itself?" ("Prophecy in Crisis: The Call of Ezekiel,"
in *Interpreting the Prophets*, edited by James L. Mays and Paul J.
Achtemeier [Philadelphia: Fortress, 1987], 157–69).

53. Chap. 23 does not include the story of the woman's marriage and
rise to fame; it simply presupposes this information and proceeds to

elaborate on the sordid details of her downfall. Neither does the chapter have anything to say about the possibility of reconciliation and good fortunes (cf. 16:53–63).

54. Once again, the Hebrew word to describe the woman's way as whorish in *znh* (16:20, 22, 26, 28, etc.; and 23:8, 14, 29, 30, etc.).

55. It is widely believed by scholars that chaps. 1–24 of Ezekiel, which concern themselves with the sins and abominations of Jerusalem, were written prior to the Second Deportation of 587 B.C.E. The implication is that these oracles were spoken to an audience that had not yet experienced the judgment of exile, which means that the prophet would have been concerned to make his audience acutely aware of their abominations and to warn them of the consequences of their behavior.

56. This claim is made all the more probable when once considers that royal and Zion theology were closely associated with the Jerusalem cult. For a discussion of Jerusalem royal and Zion theology, see Frank M. Cross, *Canaanite Myth and Hebrew Epic* (Cambridge, Mass.: Harvard University Press, 1973), and John H. Hayes, "The Tradition of Zion's Inviolability," *JBL* 2 (1963): 419–26.

57. The kinds of questions occupying the exiles in Babylon had precisely to do with the justice of God's ways and who was to blame for Jerusalem's misfortunes (see Ezekiel 18).

Chapter 3: "Am I Not Her Husband?"
The Unpredictable and Unimaginable God

1. Some of the few places where women are mentioned are the following: in Isa 3:12 the prophet denounces the way women rule over men; in Isa 3:16–24 wealthy women are denounced for their glamorous, overindulgent dress and are threatened with scabs and nakedness as their punishment; in Amos 4:1–3 wealthy women who oppress the poor and dominate their husbands are condemned and threatened with exile and humiliation; in Jer 44:15–19 women are rebuked for pouring libations for the Queen of Heaven; and in Ezek 8:14–15 women are condemned for weeping ritually for the fertility deity Tammuz.

2. For example, in Hos 4:13 the prophet denounces idolatrous practices taking place on the tops of mountains and on hills, charging that daughters and daughters-in-law engage in illicit sexual practices.

Elsewhere, in Micah 7:2–7 the prophet bewails the absence of honorable dealings, both in the public realm of civil leaders and in the private realm of family relations (i.e., sons and fathers, daughters and mothers, daughters-in-law and mothers-in-law). The prophets Isaiah and Jeremiah speculated on the future of Israel's gender relations in two curious but hopelessly obscure passages: in Isa 4:1, as part of God's judgment, there will be one man to seven women; and in Jer 31:22, as part of God's consolation to a bereaved nation, a woman will come to "protect" (?) or "surround" (?) a man.

3. Numerous studies have appeared lately examining the influence of sex and sexuality, the body and erotica on the Jewish literary imagination. The literature has covered the span of time from the biblical period to the early Zionist movement and on into contemporary American Jewish culture. Two works that have been especially illuminating and provocative are David Biale, *Eros and the Jews: From Biblical Israel to Contemporary America* (New York: Basic Books, 1992), and *The Savage in Judaism: An Anthropology of Israelite Religion and Ancient Judaism,* edited by Howard Eilberg-Schwartz (Bloomington: Indiana University Press, 1990).

4. Biale, *Eros and the Jews,* 5.

5. This is not a new proposal. The literary critic Mieke Bal has argued persuasively that instead of politics and war as the centripetal themes of Judges, sexual violence against women should be understood as the countercohering theme of the entire book. Preoccupied as the narrative is with violence in the domestic lives of men and women, the book of Judges, argues Bal, reflects a period of social revolution in Israel when concern over marriage, relations between men and women, sexuality, procreation, and kinship was acute (*Death and Dissymetry: The Politics of Coherence in the book of Judges* [Chicago: University of Chicago Press, 1988]). What I am proposing here is to see sexuality as it manifests itself in disputes about kinship, boundaries, procreation, and identity as the countercohering theme of the entire Old Testament. This, of course, remains to be proved. That may well be the subject of a later volume.

6. My own thinking about metaphors and divine judgment was stimulated by Judith Plaskow, whose work, it seems to me, always touches in some way on the relationship between evil, suffering, and injustice, on the one hand, and religious experience, on the other. In particular, her article "Facing the Ambiguity of God" (*Tikkun* 6/5 [1993]: 70f.)

stimulated my thinking about metaphors for God that acknowledge our ambivalent, oftentimes harrowing experience of the divine. Other writers have written on this topic, but no one better captured my own dissatisfaction with traditional feminist reimaginings of God than Plaskow. She writes, "How do we name the power in the world that makes us know our vulnerability, that terrifies and overwhelms us?" (p. 96). Plaskow takes this topic up in greater detail in her book *Standing Again at Sinai: Judaism from a Feminist Perspective* (New York: Harper & Row, 1990).

7. See, e.g., Jer 29:11; Ezek 18:1–32; cf. Isa 45:9–17.

8. I have elected in this case to depart from the NRSV translation and have chosen the RSV translation, whose gendered translation aptly suits the point.

9. The sage of Proverbs commented on the unpredictable, erratic side of intimacy: "Three things are too wonderful for me; / four I do not understand: / The way of an eagle in the sky, / the way of a snake on a rock, / the way of a ship on the high seas, / and the way of a man with a girl" (Prov 30:18, 19). This same unpredictable side to romance (amusing even, although that was not its focus in the prophets) was at stake in the Song of Songs. There we see the private sentiments and cryptic passions of an unknown couple, a black-skinned Shulammite maiden and her anonymous shepherd lover. We witness the drama of an intimate relationship that is never satisfying, always shrouded in uncertainty. For more discussion on this topic, see my commentary "The Song of Songs," in *New Interpreter's Bible* (Nashville: Abingdon, forthcoming).

10. In parent–child relations, too, intense emotions threaten to undermine the stability and "logic" of the relationship. Unlike judges and kings, whose offices require them to remain objective and impartial in their judgments, parents, like spouses, are understandably incapable of impartiality and detachment. Parenting, like marriage, is filled with anxiety and uncertainty. Parents invariably anguish over what to do with their children when rules are broken and expectations are unmet. In both marriage and parent–child relations, there is a realm of unspoken, intangible, unmentionable feelings and expectations that are inherent to relationships based on intimacy and kinship. In the Old Testament, God the divine parent is as personally affected by Israel's deeds—in that the parent laments, agonizes over, and is desperate to

forgive (Hosea 11)—as is God the husband. Both are torn in their emotions, and both are apt to abandon all reason and react hastily and harshly.

11. Evidently, some measures were taken from time to time to protect wives from being falsely accused of adultery by jealous husbands: for example, the ritual drink concocted in Num 5:11–31 to acquit innocent wives and to expose guilty wives. According to this story, upon drinking the drink a woman's body will give her sin away because her uterus prolapses and she becomes unable to conceive.

12. Sallie McFague, *Metaphorical Theology: Models of God in Religious Language* (Philadelphia: Fortress, 1982), 17.

13. See Howard Eilberg-Schwartz, *God's Phallus: And Other Problems for Men and Monotheism* (Boston: Beacon Press, 1994).

14. For one of the more recent discussions of monotheism in Israel, see Baruch Halpern, "'Brisker Pipes than Poetry': The Development of Israelite Monotheism," in *Judaic Perspectives on Ancient Israel*, edited by Jacob Neusner et al. (Philadelphia: Fortress, 1987). There is considerable disagreement among scholars about when Israel became monotheistic in its worship. For example, Bernhard Lang argues for a ninth-century date (*Monotheism and the Prophetic Minority* [Sheffield: Almond, 1983]), whereas Jeffrey Tigay says that monotheism was present before the ninth century, *You Shall Have No Other Gods: Israelite Religion in the Light of Hebrew Inscriptions* [Atlanta: Scholars Press, 1986]). There existed throughout Israel's history—certainly down to the fifth century—a variety of worship forms that evolved over centuries, monotheistic worship being only one that eventually won out over the others as the result of a number of political, economic, social, and theological factors.

15. The first commandment reads "you shall have no other gods before me" (Exod 20:3; cf. Deut 6:13).

16. Many feminists have devoted considerable effort to examining and rethinking the effects of monotheism on the development of Jewish and Christian religions, on the structuring of gender relations, and on questions of theodicy. Two of the most compelling feminist critiques of monotheism, written by Jewish women, are Judith Plaskow, *Standing Again at Sinai* (pp. 150–52), and Tikva Frymer-Kensky, *In the Wake of the Goddess: Women, Culture, and the Biblical Transformation of Pagan Myth* (New York: Free Press, 1992), 83–89.

17. Plaskow, "Facing the Ambiguity of God," 71.

18. I want to thank my colleague Sallie McFague for helping me think about how, why, and where the Bible is totally unilluminating, frequently confusing, and downright distressing in what it says about suffering and evil. It is disturbing to me to have to admit how much as a scholar of the Bible I have been shaped by the biblical view of suffering and evil and am sometimes unable to abandon that view for more modern, illumined ways of thinking about the topic.

Chapter 4: "Yet I Will Remember My Covenant with You"
The World of Romance and Rape

1. I am aware that the first encounter ancient audiences had with the speeches of prophets was as oral events, whether the speaker was the prophet himself or disciples who recapitulated or "read" the prophet's message to later audiences. Reading as we know it is in fact a very modern way of encountering and receiving religious instruction. As I mentioned earlier in this study, reading and readers are spoken of here advisedly so as to take advantage of some insights from reader reception theories about the way audiences receive, interact with, and negotiate meaning from "texts."

2. Feminist critics have been asking for decades how women readers read androcentric, misogynistic texts. For an excellent collection of essays that explore the ways in which women read texts written by men and women, see *Gender and Reading: Essays on Readers, Texts, and Contexts*, edited by Elizabeth A. Flynn and Patrocinio P. Schweickart (Baltimore: John Hopkins University Press, 1986). Only in recent years have serious attempts been made to ask about the effects of androcentric thinking on men and the way they read.

3. Carol Meyers's call for greater awareness of women's sphere of influence and power during the settlement period is well taken (see *Discovering Eve: Ancient Israelite Women in Context* [New York: Oxford University Press, 1988]), but this influence appears to have been limited and short-lived. Meyers admits that by the time of the monarchy, the pressures of urbanization and a centralized government resulted in a chasm between the private and the public domain: Hebrew women were relegated to the private sphere of domesticity, and their roles were subordinated to men, who ruled the public sphere.

4. Tikva Frymer-Kensky, *In the Wake of the Goddess: Women, Culture,*

and the Biblical Transformation of Pagan Myth (New York: Free Press, 1992), 128.

5. I am not claiming here that the world of the Old Testament and that of ancient Israel were exactly parallel such that we can simply infer the social world of the latter from the former. The point here rather is that to the extent that texts must have some basis in reality in order to be understood by their audience, and given that the overwhelming evidence of the Old Testament points to a world of women's subjugation, it is likely that the marital drama the prophets proposed in the marriage metaphor was one conceivable and familiar to their audiences. It is possible but unlikely that the writers were not reinforcing notions everyone already took for granted but were instead craftily trying to promote a way of viewing and treating women that was unlike what their audience knew. But the situation of women was not really the point of the marriage metaphor. The logic of viewing and treating (adulterous) women in Hebrew society in a certain way is appealed to only insofar as it helps to shed light on the lesser-understood concept of how and why God views and treats Israel in certain ways.

6. The latter can be seen in the law governing the rape of unbetrothed virgins in Deut 22:28–29. According to this law, the penalty for raping an unbetrothed virgin was to compensate her father with fifty shekels of silver for the loss of his property. The rapist was then mandated to marry his rape victim.

7. For an important work on the impalpable effects androcentric writings have upon women readers and the ways in which women attempt to "resist" their series of designs, see Judith Fetterly, The Resisting Reader: A Feminist Approach to American Fiction (Bloomington: Indiana University Press, 1978).

8. Women such as the wise woman of Tekoa (2 Samuel 14), the wise woman at Abel (2 Sam 20:14–22), the daughters of Zelophehad (Num 27:1–11), and the prophet Huldah (2 Kgs 22:11–20) were well aware of the power of rhetoric and the hold words can have upon the imagination. Huldah, for example, was consulted and asked to exegete the law scroll placed before her because no one knew better than prophets like herself that all literature, even religious literature, deserves careful scrutiny.

9. Unlike her predecessor Dinah in Genesis 34, who presumably was raped before she could speak and protest, Tamar in 2 Sam 13:1–39 tries

to reason with her would-be rapist, her step-brother Amnon. She employs her own rhetoric of resistance, petition, shame, and honor to persuade Amnon not to rape her, but her resistance fails.

10. See J. Cheryl Exum's provocative discussion of how efficient literary rape can be in objectifying women in "Raped by the Pen," in *Fragmented Women: Feminist (Sub)versions of Biblical Narratives* (Valley Forge, Penn.: Trinity Press International, 1993), 170–201.

11. My thinking about the need to break the hold texts have over the imagination by reading them in ways in which they were not meant to be read owes a lot to Adrienne Rich's discussion of feminist literary criticism, especially in an article that has become a classic discussion on the topic, "When We Dead Awaken: Writing as Re-vision," in *On Lies, Secrets, and Silence: Selected Prose 1966-1978* (New York: Norton, 1979). "We need to know the writing of the past," Rich writes, "and know it differently than we have ever known it; not to pass on a tradition but to break its hold over us" (p. 35).

12. Of course, there is the matter of the potentially ironic inference of *pth*, meaning "to lure" or "to seduce." While the tone of the entire pericope suggests that the verb is probably referring to the simple romantic act of wooing and flattering, there are occasions in the Old Testament when this verb connotes deception, as in the story of Delilah and Samson (Judg 14:15; 16:5) and God's deception of King Ahab (1 Kgs 22:20).

13. It is interesting to note that "love" is nowhere mentioned in 2:4–23. The man's interests are not so much in restoring love as in reclaiming property and showing up his wife's lovers: "She herself did not know that it was I who gave her the grain, the wine, and the oil, and lavished upon her silver and gold which they used for Baal" (2:8).

14. Chapters 30–31 of Jeremiah, usually seen as an independent cycle of oracles, have been designated variously as "the book of consolation," "the book of restoration," or "the little book of hope."

15. The exact meaning of the expression "a female surrounds a warrior" is unclear. Kathleen O'Connor makes several proposals, "Perhaps it refers to future sexual relationships in which women will be active agents in the procreation of a restored people. Perhaps it speaks of a society at peace so that women will be capable of protecting warriors. Or perhaps it anticipates role reversals of a different sort. What is clear

is that the surprising new role of women symbolizes a changed order of relationships in a reconstituted and joyous society" ("Jeremiah, the Book of," in *The Women's Bible Commentary*, edited by Carol A. Newsom and Sharon H. Ringe [Louisville: Westminster/John Knox, 1992], 176).

16. According to Ezekiel, a generation of readers emerged during the exile who indeed did question the kind of divine justice attested to in speeches like those in chaps. 16 and 23. The exiles' response to such thinking was simple and to the point: "The way of the Lord is unfair" (18:25, 29). Ezekiel argues for individual versus group retribution in quoting the exiles' complaint against God. But the statement could just as well have been a popular complaint throughout the exilic period, dating as far back as the destruction of Jerusalem.

17. The prophet carefully avoids any suggestion that the husband rapes the wife. That is because God, though gendered in the Bible as male, is absolutely never represented as acting sexually. While the metaphor builds upon sensual and romantic language, the marriage metaphor avoids any allusion to God actually engaging in sexual intercourse. There are descriptions of God wooing, pleading, seducing, talking sweetly, and lavishing gifts, but never of God making love with Israel (see Frymer-Kensky, *In the Wake of the Goddess*, 188–89).

18. In my earlier article "Gomer: Victim of Violence or Victim of Metaphor," I certainly couldn't bring myself to consider the metaphor as having any redeemable value. I ponder the possibility even now with great apprehension.

19. Katheryn Pfisterer Darr approaches this same topic from a different point of view; she raises the pedagogical question about how to teach what she calls "troubling texts" (she includes a study of Ezekiel 16). See her "Ezekiel's Justification of God: Teaching Troubling Texts," *JSOT* 55 (1992): 87–117.

20. My comments here are greatly influenced by Patrocinio Schweickart's excellent theoretical analysis of the ways in which women read writings by men. See her often-cited article on this topic, "Toward A Feminist Theory of Reading," in *Gender and Reading: Essays on Readers, Texts, and Contexts*, 31–62.

21. This latter hermeneutical strategy is closely akin to what Elisabeth Schüssler Fiorenza refers to as a "hermeneutics of re-vision."

See "Transforming the Legacy," in *Searching the Scriptures: A Feminist Introduction*, edited by Elisabeth Schüssler Fiorenza (New York: Crossroad, 1993), 11.

22. Mary Ann Tolbert, "Defining the Problem: The Bible and Feminist Hermeneutics," *Semeia* 28 (1983): 120.

23. Jeremiah's "Temple Sermon" in chap. 7 is perhaps a good example of the drama and elocution the prophets exerted to capture Israel's attention. Here the prophet Jeremiah comes across as confident and unwavering in his office, but there is plenty of evidence in his laments that the prophet was plagued with doubt, disappointment, and disgust at the hostility and skepticism his prophecies met (11:18–12:6; 15:10–21; 17:14–18; 18:18–23; 20:14–18).

24. This phrase is borrowed from Toni Morrison in *Playing in the Dark: Whiteness and the Literary Imagination* (Cambridge, Mass.: Harvard University Press, 1992), 15. In this study of the impact of race on the literary imagination, she discusses the crafting of a literary work, especially of the social consequences of the choices authors make, in this case the effects of race on the literary imagination.

25. There are admittedly places in the Bible so senseless in the violence imagined against women and others (e.g., the butchered concubine in Judges 19) that it feels as if the only sensible thing to do as a reader would be to stop reading the Bible altogether.

26. Acutely aware of the ability of language and metaphors to shape reality, Drorah Setel insists correctly: "The sexes of Gomer and Hosea and their respective behavior are not a random representation but a reflection and reinforcement of cultural perceptions. Hence, Hosea's metaphor has both theological and social meaning. With regard to theological understanding, it indicates that God has the authority of possession and control over Israel that a husband has over a wife. The reverse of the representation is a view of human males as being analogous to Yahweh, while women are comparable to the people, who by definition, are subservient to Yahweh's will. . . . A central issue for contemporary religious feminists is the extent to which the use of these (and other) biblical writings continues to so define women in our own societies" ("Prophets and Pornography: Female Sexual Imagery in Hosea," in *Feminist Interpretation of the Bible*, edited by Letty Russell [Philadelphia: Westminster, 1985], 93, 95).

27. Paul Ricoeur stresses the paradoxical nature of metaphorical

speech (*The Rule of Metaphor* [Toronto: University of Toronto Press, 1977], 7).

28. I owe a lot of my thinking about our culture as brokenhearted and in pain to the marvelous work of Rita Nakashima Brock, *Journeys by Heart: A Christology of Erotic Power* (New York: Crossroad, 1993). Her theological examination of the erotic (drawing from Audre Lorde, Susan Griffin, and Adrienne Rich) as a source of healing power from within the heart has pushed me to reexamine the marriage metaphor as a potential source for imagining and talking theologically about matters of heartfelt importance (e.g., family, love, children, intimacy, relationships).

29. One might reasonably ask whether our sympathies have to be with one and not the other. Is it possible to be sympathetic toward both? Of course, this does not help us with the original proposition the drama sets up: the wife is the one who is to blame for the whole sordid affair. No explanation is given in patriarchal thinking about what drove the wife to become involved in these illicit affairs.

30. The subject of theological models, or "metaphors with staying power," was initiated by Sallie McFague in *Metaphorical Theology* and was explored further in her recent book *Models of God: Theology for an Ecological, Nuclear Age* (Philadelphia: Fortress, 1987). In the latter work, McFague moves beyond the deconstructive work of the former book and attempts reconstructively to offer new, challenging theological metaphors (e.g., God as friend, lover, mother) in view of the ecologically diminishing context in which modern readers find themselves.

31. Abraham Heschel, *The Prophets* (New York: Harper Colophon, 1962), 9.

32. For example, the marriage metaphor elevates heterosexual relations to a paradigmatic theological insight and fails to take into account the unique insights that homosexual unions offer about love, eros, self, family, and the divine.

Index